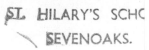

This book is due for return on or before the last date shown below.

Don Gresswell Ltd., London, N.21 Cat. No. 1208

DG 02242/71

Past-into-Present Series

THE LABOUR PARTY

Peter Lane

Principal Lecturer in History,
Coloma College of Education

B T BATSFORD LTD London

First published 1973
© Peter Lane, 1973

Typeset and printed in Great Britain by
REDWOOD BURN LIMITED
Trowbridge & Esher
for the publishers
B T Batsford Ltd, 4 Fitzhardinge Street, London W1H 0AH
ISBN 0 7134 1790 0

Acknowledgments

The Author and Publisher wish to thank the following for the illustrations which appear in this book: Barratt's for figs 31, 55; the *Daily Mail* for fig. 38; Fox Photos for fig. 51; the Illustrated London News for fig. 13; the Imperial War Museum for fig. 54; Keystone Press for figs 59, 60, 62, 64; the Labour Party for figs 25, 32, 34; Manchester City Art Gallery for fig. 9; the Mansell Collection for figs 8, 11, 14, 17, 18, 20, 27, 35, 37, 41–46; the *New Statesman* for figs 58, 63; Paul Popper Ltd for fig. 61; Radio Times Hulton Picture Library for figs 1–4, 7, 19, 33, 36, 39, 40, 47–50, 52, 56; the *Times* for fig. 53; UPI for fig. 57.

Contents

The Illustrations

Introduction

In 1924 Ramsay MacDonald became the first Labour Prime Minister. In his diary for 22 January, 1924, King George V wrote: 'At 12.15 I held a Council, at which Mr Ramsay MacDonald was sworn in as a member. I then asked him to form a government, which he accepted to do. I had an hour's talk with him, he impressed me very much; he wishes to do the right thing. Today, twenty-three years ago, dear Grandmamma died. I wonder what she would have thought of a Labour government!'

1 (*From left to right*). J. Ramsay MacDonald, the illegitimate son of a Scottish fishing girl; J. H. Thomas, an engine driver; Arthur Henderson, an iron foundry worker and J. R. Clynes, a mill hand, as they left Buckingham Palace, January 1924 after being sworn in as Privy Councillors on the formation of the first Labour government

2 The end of the Second World War. On the first Sunday after VE Day, May 1945, Winston Churchill and his wife attended the Thanksgiving Service at St Paul's Cathedral

In July 1945, the Labour Party, led by Clement Attlee, won the general election by a massive, record majority. A lady dining at Claridge's, a leading London hotel, read the result and cried out: 'They have elected a Labour government. The country will never stand for it.'

These very recent attitudes towards the Labour Party may appear strange to a generation which now looks on the Labour Party as the natural, normal alternative to the Tory Party. Why did some people have this dislike for the Labour Party? Why has this attitude died out? Why had Queen Victoria never had to deal with a Labour government? When did this Party begin and why? These are some of the questions that I have tried to answer in the following pages.

1 Early Forms of Workers' Protests

The first wage earners

Up to the twelfth century the lords of Britain's manors did not receive money rents from their tenants. Some tenants paid rent by giving their lord honey, meat, eggs, cloth and so on; others paid their rent by working for so many days a year on the lord's own farm. In the twelfth century many of the landowners began to charge money rents instead of these forced services. The lords realised that the land would be better worked by hired men working all the year round than by the grudging service provided by farmers, called from working on their own land.

The wages that the lords had to pay were fixed by Parliament or by the local Justices of the Peace, and the system seems to have worked fairly well, although there are accounts of riots by discontented workers. However, in 1348 and 1349, the Black Death swept across the country killing off about half the population. One result of this calamity was that every tenant farmer had about twice as much land to himself as he had worked previously; another was that each wage-earning labourer found that he could get higher wages from lords anxious to have their farms worked.

The custom of charging money rents had not been adopted everywhere and many tenants of 'service custom' estates fled to areas where they could have a farm without any services, or to a manor where they could earn higher wages. On some manors where money rents had become the new custom, some lords tried to turn back the clock, announcing that they had decided to end the practice and, in place of paying hired men, they expected their tenants to provide the old-fashioned payment in kind or in service.

In 1351, Edward III's Parliament passed the Statute of Labourers: 'The King to the Sheriff of Kent, greeting. Because a great part of workmen have lately died in the pestilence, many . . . will not service unless they may receive excessive wages . . . we, have upon deliberation . . . (with the nobles) assisting us, ordained . . . That every man . . . take only the wages which were accustomed to be given in the . . . twentieth year of our reign. . . . And if any such man . . . will not do the same, he shall . . . (be) committed to the next goal.' This was violently opposed by rioting workmen, local unions, and bands of outlaws, including the legendary Robin Hood.

The Peasants' Revolt, 1381

The English farmworkers were learning to oppose wage-fixing and the attempt of their lords to bring back the 'service economy' in which money had played only a small part. In the small, but growing, towns the local craftsmen (weavers, goldsmiths, tailors, carpenters and so on) were beginning to show similar signs of independence; they wanted their towns to be freed from control by the local landowners. In areas controlled by the Crown this was fairly simple; the King was usually willing to sell this freedom to the townspeople who, by a Royal Charter, became independent with their own mayor and council. In towns controlled by abbeys or bishops, the craftsmen found it more difficult to get their freedom and so there were frequent riots by respectable townspeople against their clerical overlords.

The stage seemed to be set for a conflict between the lower classes and their superiors. Onto this stage came John Ball and other friars and travelling priests preaching the message of equality. As Ball said:

> *When Adam delved and Eve span,*
> *Who was then the gentleman?*

In 1380 King Richard II's government decided to impose a poll tax: each person, irrespective of income, was to pay the same tax. This was obviously unfair since it imposed a greater hardship on the poor than on the rich. This was the spark which set alight the fires of revolution. In the South-Eastern part of England the monasteries were specially unpopular and suffered much from the violence of the rebels. The Prior of Bury St Edmunds was murdered by his own serfs. In London, Wat Tyler's men beheaded Archbishop Simon of Sudbury on Tower Hill, because as Chancellor of the realm he represented the unpopular government. In revenge, the fighting Bishop of Norwich led in person the Army which suppressed the rising in East Anglia.

Then took place the most remarkable incident of our long social history—the capture of London. Many of the village bands had been advised to march on the capital, where the popular leaders had allies. The London mob opened the gates to the rustic armies. The young King Richard saw all this from the Tower of London. As a contemporary chronicler recalled:

During this time the King, being in a turret of the great Tower of London, saw the manor of the Savoy and Clerkenwell and the houses of Simon Hosteler by Newgate and the place of John de Butterwyk in flames, and he called all the lords about him into a room and asked their advice as to what should be done in such a crisis. None of them could or would suggest anything; whereupon the young King said he would order the Mayor of the city to command the sheriffs and aldermen to have cried in their wards that everyone between

3 Wat Tyler being slain at his interview with King Richard II. The first workers' revolt came to an abrupt end in 1381

the ages of fifteen and sixty, on pain of life and limb, should be on the morrow at Mile End and meet him there at seven of the bell.

At Mile End on the following morning there took place a remarkable confrontation between the rebels, led by Wat Tyler, and King Richard. Froissart's account of the meeting includes this extract: " 'Truly,' replied the Mayor, who found himself supported by the King, 'does it become such a stinking rascal as thou art to use such speech in the presence of the King . . .? I will not live a day, if thou pay not for it.' " Wat Tyler was slain and his followers went back to their homes—the first workers' movement was over.

Early trade unions

Wat Tyler and his rebel bands had shown that they understood the nature of political power. They realised that lasting changes in their working and living conditions could come about only if the law was changed, which could not be done without the consent of the ruling class. They hoped to impose their political will

A DISCOVERY OF THE MOST
DANGEROVS AND DAMNABLE TENETS
THAT HAVE BEEN SPREAD WITHIN THIS FEW
yeares: By many Erronious, Heriticall and Mechannick ſpirits. By which the very foundation of Chriſtian knowledge
and practiſe is endeavoured to be overturned.

a Confectioner | a Smith | a Sho-maker | a Taylor
a Sadler | a Porter | a Box-maker | a Sope-boyler
a Glover | a Meal-man | a Chilk en-man | a Button-maker

4 When one group of revolutionaries beheaded Charles II other more radical groups rose up. One such group was the Levellers who wanted a communist-type government and social system. As the headline shows, not everyone shared this belief in absolute equality

on the ruling politicians. Their attempts failed and within a short period the lower orders were again under the control of their superiors.

As the old manor system had decayed, so too did the old craft system. Once upon a time a boy became an apprentice and after years of training became a qualified craftsman. For a time he worked for a master craftsman until he had saved enough to buy himself the tools of his trade and then he, too, set up as a master craftsman, taking on apprentices and paying recently qualified craftsmen to work for him. In the sixteenth and seventeenth centuries the master craftsmen made it increasingly difficult for others to become masters; they put up the fees that had to be paid before a person became a master and they insisted that they must buy expensive gowns. This, and the growing cost of the tools of the trade, meant that many qualified craftsmen could never hope to rise from the ranks of wage-earning employees. There are many examples of these journeymen (or daily-paid) wage-earners forming their own trade unions to try to obtain better conditions for themselves.

In 1623 the textile weavers of Wiltshire appealed to the local Justices of the Peace to change the wage rates because of those 'that are not able by their diligent labours to get their living, by reasons that the clothiers . . . have abated wages what they please. May it please you therefore . . . to appoint certain persons . . . to assess rates for wages . . . that the poor artificers of these works of woollen cloth may not perish for want of food'.

In 1696 the journeymen feltmakers of London announced that they had 'come to a resolution among themselves not to accept of any less wages for making of hats than what they formerly received'.

The journeymen were obviously getting bolder. Whereas once they had asked the Justices to fix their wages, by the early eighteenth century they were confronting the employers with demands for higher wages, without any consultation with the local Justices as required by law.

In 1721 the master tailors of London asked Parliament to pass a law against this practice. Their petition gives a good indication of the nature of these early trade unions. They complained of the weavers that:

the number of seven thousand and upwards have lately entered into a combination to raise their wages and leave off working an hour sooner than they used to do; and for the better carrying on their design, have subscribed their respective names in books prepared for that purpose, at public houses in and about Lon-

5 The domestic system, or cottage industry, in the years before the invention of the steam engine and the growth of the factory system. 'Every cottage had its wheel and every village its loom'. In this system there was little chance of workers forming trade unions and since most people lived in villages there was little chance of a working-class political movement

don and Westminster. At this time there are but few of them come to work at all, and most of those that do, insist upon twelve shillings and ninepence (64p) per week [instead of ten shillings and ninepence (54p) per week, the usual wages] and leave off work at eight of the clock at night [instead of nine, their usual hour] . . . [they are also engaged in] collecting great sums of money to support their unlawful combinations. [They] are of very ill example to journeymen in other trades; as is sufficiently seen in the journeymen curriers, smiths, farriers, sail-makers, coach-makers, who have joined into [unions] of the like nature; the journeymen carpenters, bricklayers and joiners have taken some steps for that purpose, and only wait to see the [success] of others.

Non-political unions

These early trade unions were concerned with the wages, hours and working conditions of their members. They were also interested in acting as a welfare society on behalf of their members. The *House of Commons' Journal* notes:

13 March 1794. Report on Woolcombers' Petition.
William Gates being asked whether it was usual to go from place to place to seek employment, he said it was, and that their clubs or societies subsist them till they get work . . . And being asked, whether there are any number of wool-combers who do not belong to the societies, he said, 'There are some, but not one in one hundred that does not belong to some society'.

Jonathan Sowton . . . was asked, of what nature the clubs were. He said, 'It is a contribution upon which every woolcomber (who is willing to be a member of a club) . . . the one end of it is to enable the woolcombers to travel from place to place to seek for employment, when work is scarce where he resides; and the other end of it is to have relief when he is sick wherever he may be; and if he should die, to be buried by the club; . . . it is necessary for him, to entitle himself to be relieved by these clubs, to have a certificate from the club to which he belongs, that he has behaved well in and to the woolcombing trade, and that he is an honest man'.

But no government was prepared to allow these unions to flourish. This hostile attitude was strengthened when the French Revolution showed what might happen if the mob were allowed a free hand. In 1799 the government passed the first of the Combination Acts, which said that all contracts made by journeymen or other workmen for obtaining an advance of wages or for lessening their usual hours or time of working, were illegal. Workmen making such agreements were liable to three month's imprisonment in a common gaol or two months in a house of correction.

Industrial change

The unions which were attacked by the Combination Acts were different to the

6 An early trade union card which shows the pride of the workman in his craft

earlier unions of the seventeenth century. They were the product of the industrial changes which had begun to alter the face of Britain as early as the middle of the eighteenth century. In 1750 Norwich and Bristol had been the country's largest towns outside London—and their populations were about 40,000. By 1800 there were dozens of towns larger than these, as a result of the development of coal-mining, iron-making, factory-based cotton manufacture and weaving, the growth of engineering and other industries. For the first time many thousands of people came together in unhealthy, industrial towns.

Reactions by the workers

Some workers merely wanted to halt the process by which their standards of living were being attacked. Led by the mythical Ned Ludd, the Luddites smashed machines, burned factories and killed industrialists in the hope that this would bring back the 'golden age' when they had been free of the tyranny of the machine.

Others, under the influence of radical politicians, realised that they were not going to be able to halt the process of industrialisation. They realised that they would gain more by co-operating with the process which was making the country much wealthier. They realised that if they could gain a share of this increased wealth—in higher wages, improved housing, better clothes and so on—their lives would be more pleasant than those of their grandparents. This led some of them to support the movement in favour of parliamentary reform.

2 Industrial Change and Workers' Politics, 1830–1870

The industrial changes which began in the eighteenth century made Britain the richest country in the world and her industrialists, merchants, financiers and professional men became the rich middle class described by Galsworthy in the *Forsyte Saga*. The landed aristocrats who ruled the country realised that they would have to change the political system to allow this new class to share in the government of the country, and in 1832 the first Reform Act was passed, ending the domination of the landed class who, in future, would have to share their political power with the new industrialists.

7 Even at the end of the nineteenth century there were millions of poor people in Britain. This picture, taken in Liverpool in 1895, shows just two of the many thousands of boys who dressed in rags and went barefooted to school

Robert Owen

However, the Reform Act did nothing for the workers; nor did the reformed Parliament do much to make life any better for them. Robert Owen, a Welsh industrialist, believed that life could be improved. In 1800 he took over the cotton mills at New Lanark where, as he wrote:

I entered upon the government of New Lanark about 1 January 1800 ... My intention was ... to change the conditions of the people, who were surrounded by circumstances having an injurious influence upon the character of the entire population of New Lanark.

... I arranged superior stores and shops from which to supply every article of food, clothing etc which they required. I bought everything with money in the first markets, and contracted for fuel, milk, etc. on a large scale, and had the whole of these articles of the best qualities supplied to the people at cost price ... The effects soon became visible in their improved health and superior dress, and in the general comfort of their houses.

Owen was very modern in his outlook—in his belief that man's environment is important. His experience in New Lanark helped him to develop his ideas on socialism—a word which he introduced into the English language in 1827. Owen wrote:

It is well known that during the last half century, Great Britain ... increased its power of production; the natural effect of the aid thus obtained from science

8 Robert Owen, who first used the word 'socialism'

16

9 This painting, *Work*, by Ford Madox Ford illustrates the romantic idea that many Victorians had about the dignity of work. The middle class and many of the skilled working class believed that work would bring rewards for everyone. The less well-to-do would not have agreed; they knew the penalties of low wages, frequent unemployment and industrial accidents

should be to add to the wealth and happiness of society . . . and that all parties would thereby be substantially benefited . . . On the contrary . . . the working classes, which form so large a proportion of the population cannot obtain even the comforts which their labour formerly procured for them.

Already in 1821 he had realised that the greater wealth of the country was falling into the hands of too few people, while the mass of the people were no better off as a result of this increase in the nation's wealth. Owen believed that it was possible to organise society so that the wealth would be more fairly shared out. But his ideas were not popular with the ruling class who had gained a great deal from the industrial changes.

17

Trade unionism

Nor did Owen's ideas appeal to the working classes. They preferred to rely on the activities of their unions to bargain with employers so that wage rates could be pushed up, enabling men to buy for themselves a fairer share of the world's goods. In 1834 Owen adopted the idea of forming a Grand National Consolidated Trades Union for all the workers in the country. At first the idea caught on and soon he had 500,000 members. But the success was superficial. Few of the skilled workers joined, preferring their own, smaller, select unions for carpenters, weavers and so on. Most of Owen's members were unskilled workers who could not afford the fees which his union required if it was to work properly. Owen believed that it was possible to persuade the ruling class to change their policies by peaceful means; all that had to be done, he thought, was to argue, write, debate and otherwise show them what was wrong with their present policies and how life could be improved. Other leaders of the GNCTU thought that force was required and that, at the very least, a national general strike should be called to bring the country's industry to a halt. This, they thought, would persuade the government and employers to change their policies.

In fact, neither Owen nor his opponents were right. Certainly employers were not persuaded that the socialist ideas of Owen or his union should be supported. They compelled workmen to sign a document promising not to support Owen or his union; anyone refusing to do so was sacked. If someone tried to form a union, local magistrates, with the support of the government, invoked laws under which prosecutions could take place. The most famous example of this method of stamping on trade union growth was that which took place at Tolpuddle when six farmers were sentenced to transportation for trying to form a branch of the GNCTU.

Co-operation

Robert Owen's ideas on trade unionism were no more successful than his attempts to persuade the world to adopt a socialist policy. One legacy he did leave to Victorian workmen was the idea of co-operative buying and selling. This idea was adopted by a group of workmen at Rochdale who, in 1844, opened the first Co-operative Store. As the *History of the Rochdale Pioneers* recalls:

> The objects of this Society are to form arrangements for the pecuniary benefit and improvement of the social and domestic condition of its members, by raising a sufficient amount of capital, in shares of one pound each, to bring into operation the following plans and arrangements:
>
> The establishment of a store for the sale of provisions, clothing, etc; the building, purchasing, or erecting a number of houses, in which those members desiring to assist each other in improving their domestic and social condition may reside; to commence the manufacture of such articles as the Society may

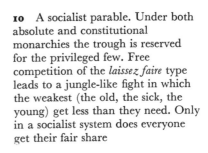

10 A socialist parable. Under both absolute and constitutional monarchies the trough is reserved for the privileged few. Free competition of the *laissez faire* type leads to a jungle-like fight in which the weakest (the old, the sick, the young) get less than they need. Only in a socialist system does everyone get their fair share

determine upon, for the employment of such members as may be without employment, or who may be suffering in consequence of repeated reductions in their wages.

Chartism

The GNCTU failed to achieve anything; meanwhile, workmen continued to work long hours for low wages and, with their families, suffered a very poor standard of living. In the late 1830s this already low standard was threatened by an economic depression in which many thousands were thrown out of work, while millions had to accept cuts in wages. These were the factors which drove many workmen in different parts of the country to turn once again to politics as a possible solution to the evils that affected them.

In many towns and villages, particularly in the North of England and in South Wales, groups of workmen met to form a Chartist Society cell. They held mass meetings in which they preached the advantage of political reform, and many produced their own charters. Delegates from local associations went to meetings in Manchester, Bristol and other centres claiming to speak for hundreds of thousands of Chartist members, and in 1838 William Lovett, a London journeyman cabinet-maker produced a charter which outlined the six main points common to most of the charters. This was presented to Parliament in 1839:

> That it might please their honourable house to take the petition into their most serious consideration, and to use their utmost endeavour to pass a law, granting to every man of lawful age, sound mind and uncontaminated by crime, the right of voting for Members to serve in Parliament; that they would also cause a law to be passed, giving the right of vote by ballot; that the duration of Parliament might in no case be of greater duration than one year; that they would abolish all property qualifications, to entitle persons to sit in their honourable House; and that all Members elected to sit in Parliament, should be paid for their services.

The Petition was rejected by a Parliament of rich men who did not wish to see their powers or privileges attacked. In 1842, and again in 1848, the Chartists marched, demonstrated and handed in petitions—but to no avail.

Individualism

Both Robert Owen's socialism and the Chartists' hopes that Parliament would pass laws making life better for the working class ran against the tide of opinion in Victorian Britain. This was the age of self-help as preached by Samuel Smiles:

> The greatest results in life are usually attained by simple means and . . . ordinary qualities. The common life of every day, with its cares, necessities, and duties,

11 *A Chartist meeting*, by S. P. Fletcher. Most Chartist meetings were held out of doors—they had insufficient money to hire halls. This night-time meeting is going to be addressed by one of the respectably-dressed riders; most of the Chartists here and nationally were from the working classes. Notice the weapons; many people feared that Chartism would lead to a bloody revolution

12 This cartoon from *Punch*, 1848, shows Lord John Russell (who had introduced the first Reform Act in 1831–32) being presented with the Charter signed by many millions of supporters. *Punch* may have believed that the demands were not unreasonable; Lord John Russell, however, had said that the 1832 Act was the 'final solution' to the reform of Parliament. 'Finality Jack' as he was called, shared the belief of the majority of upper- and middle-class people in Britain that Chartism was a dangerous menace

affords . . . opportunity for acquiring experience of the best kind; and its most beaten paths provide the worker with scope for effort and self-improvement. The high-road of human welfare lies along the highway of steadfast well-doing; and they who are the most persistent . . . will be the most successful.

Every man was supposed to be able to look after himself; he did not need Parliament to look after him.

It is easy to see that self-help appealed to the landowners, whose rent rolls grew as towns were built on their land. The middle classes also gained from the industrialisation which produced ever growing profits for factory owners and railway owners, for bankers and merchants, for engineers and contractors. Many of these people learned to imitate the life styles of their social superiors, building their own country and town houses, employing their armies of servants and sending their children away to boarding schools.

Workers and individualism

Even the skilled workers supported the idea of self-help. By 1870 the skilled craftsmen of Victorian England were earning £2 and £3 per week—which is a miserable pittance compared to the £12,000 a year which Gladstone took in rents from his estate at Hawarden, but was a considerable improvement on the 10s (50p) a week which the workers earned in the 1830s.

At the same time prices had fallen considerably, so that Robert Giffen wrote in 1877:

13 The interior of a Durham miner's cottage, 1893. Here you can see the comparative comfort of the skilled worker's home which is well furnished and decorated. Compare the child here with the children of unskilled workmen in Picture 7

14 *Capital and Labour*: a *Punch* cartoon, 1843. At the top of the cartoon you can see the type of life led by the successful industrialist, with servants, good food and drink and a pampered pet monkey (right). Below you can see the workers and their families who have produced the wealth which is being enjoyed by the industrialist and his family

The working classes have enjoyed a great improvement in wages in the last fifty years ... estimated at 50 to 100 per cent ... [There has been a] fall in the prices of the principal articles of general consumption, which left to the labourer a large margin for increased [expenditure], ... The condition of the masses has in fact improved vastly, as is shown by the diminished rate of mortality, the increased consumption per head of tea, sugar, and the like articles ... What has happened to the working classes ... is a revolution, having substituted, for millions of people ... who were constantly on the brink of starvation and who suffered untold privations, new millions of artisans and fairly well-paid labourers.

These skilled craftsmen's suspicions of socialism and Chartism had been confirmed by the failure of Owen and the collapse of Chartism. In the early 1850s they set out to establish their own national unions, amalgamating local societies into national societies such as the Amalgamated Society of Engineers (1851), which in 1867 told the Royal Commission on Trade Unions:

23

The Society was formed in 1851 of a number of societies which had previously existed, and it now numbered 33,000 members, with an annual increase of 2,000 or 3,000 a year. There are 308 branches . . . All these branches are governed by one code of rules . . . Each member pays 1s [5p] a week and the society has now a fund in different banks, in round numbers, of £140,000. The annual income in 1865 was £86,885, made up, besides subscriptions, of entrance fees, each member having to pay an entrance fee varying from 15s [75p] to £3 10s [£3.50]. The expenditure in 1865 was £49,172, the heads under which it was distributed being—members out of employment, £14,076; to sick members £13,788 14s 9d [£13,788.74]; superannuated members (members who are 'too old to gain the ordinary rate of wages at the trade' being allowed 7s to 9s [35p to 45p] a week each), £5,184, 17s 4d [£5,184.72]; on the death of members and members' wives, £4,887; and the sum of £1,800 among 18 members

15 Rioting in Hyde Park, 4 August 1866. Palmerston had died in 1865 and the movement for Parliamentary Reform took on a new lease of life. John Bright persuaded Gladstone to support the demands of workingmen for the right to vote. His Bill was defeated by a combination of Tories and right-wing Whigs led by Robert Lowe. There were demonstrations in many parts of the country when this news was announced and here you can see a contemporary drawing of the violent demonstration in London. Oddly enough in 1867 the Tories were persuaded by Disraeli that it would be a good idea to introduce a Reform Bill, and this became the Second Reform Act, 1867, which gave some workingmen the right to vote—and so paved the way for the Labour Party to come into existence

THE RIOT IN HYDE PARK.

who met with accidents and were unable to follow the trade. Then there is a benevolent fund, made up of a compulsory levy on every member. It should here be remarked that a member, on ceasing for any reason to be a member, loses all these benefits, except those who have received the injury money, and they are entitled to the benefits on paying 6d [2½p] a week.

Here were all the advantages of self-help. These men's skills earned them high wages so that they could buy their own houses (through one or other of the building societies for the working classes), or rent one of the thousands of new homes being built on the outskirts of the growing towns. Their wives dressed well, their families enjoyed an occasional day at the seaside or in the country; they ate well, they joined one of the workingmen's clubs where they read, debated, listened to lectures and, in general, behaved in a way which marked them off from the great mass of the working class who, unskilled and low-paid, lived lives of desperate poverty.

Skilled workers and politics

The Second Reform Act (1867) gave the right to vote to any adult male householder living in a parliamentary borough. The electorate was almost doubled, with nearly 300,000 new names being added to the voting register. Working-class voters now formed a clear majority over the middle classes in the towns.

How did the working-class voters use this power which had been one of the Chartists' demands? In many places they formed Tory Workingmen's Associations. In other places they formed Liberal Workingmen's Associations—although the Liberal Party was the political home of their employers. Two trade union leaders, Thomas Burt and Alexander Macdonald, were adopted by local Liberal Associations as parliamentary candidates, and after 1874 they sat in the Commons as working-class members of the Liberal Party, earning for themselves the nickname Lib/Labs.

Neither Burt nor Macdonald thought that it was any part of their task to represent the working classes; they were there to speak for trade unionism only. The fact that neither Tory nor Liberal governments did much to change the pattern of life for the unskilled masses was nothing to do with the Lib/Labs who dominated the trade union movement.

3   The People of the Abyss

The upper working class

In 1870 about one million working men earned between £2 and £3 a week and bought for themselves a high standard of living. They felt at one with their employers, many of whom had themselves been working men. If these could claw their way out of the ranks of the workers so too, it seemed, could others. As one song of 1867 went:

> *Work, boys, work and be contented*
> *So long as you've enough to buy a meal;*
> *The man you may rely*
> *Will be wealthy by and by*
> *If he'll only put his shoulder to the wheel.*

The unskilled worker

A Royal Commission on Labour, set up in 1892, heard evidence that the minimum wage required for a man, wife and two children, was 30s [£1.50] a week. This argument was put forward by H. M. Hyndman, an old Etonian who had become a Marxist Socialist. He outlined a budget for this ideal family: [5p = 12d *or* 1s]

	s	d	
Rent	5	3	(three rooms, if lucky)
Firing	2	9½	
Light		8½	
Soap, soda etc		10	
Bread	1	8	(slightly under four quartern loaves, at 5½d)
Oatmeal		4	
Grocery	2	6	(tea at 4s a lb; sugar at 2d)
Butter,			(cheese at 7¼d a lb;
cheese etc	1	0	butter at 1/3d a lb.)
Flour		4	
Meat	3	0	
Vegetables			(potatoes at ½d a lb.)
and Fruit	2	6	
Club, union,			
sickness &			
death benefit	3	3	
Total	25	2	

16 The demonstration of the unemployed, February 1886. The mob can be seen charging down St James's Street, London; they attacked rich men's clubs and the fashionable shops, as well as the army and police who were sent in to disperse them. This, and similar demonstrations led by members of the Socialist Democratic Federation, resulted in Burns and others being taken to court

The remaining 4s 10d would have had to cover everything else—clothes, furniture, repairs, recreation, books and so on. It is obvious that this was the budget of people living at a low standard, but Robert Giffen, the leading Victorian economist, estimated that just over 80 per cent (or 4 out of every 5) of the working men earned less than this.

Some families had a low income because of unemployment. As Ben Tillett recalled, the London dockers frequently found it impossible to get work: 'To obtain employment we are driven into a shed, iron-barred from end to end, outside of which a foreman or contractor walks up and down with the air of a dealer in a cattle market, picking and choosing from a crowd of men, who in their eagerness to obtain employment trample each other underfoot, and where like beasts they fight for a day's work'.

When these men did get work the employers offered only low wages. London tramway drivers in 1898, working 16 hours a day, earned 15p a day, and so could not get more than £2.05 even if they worked 7 days a week. In 1896 Ernest Bevin, who later became a leading trade unionist, and MP and Foreign Secretary, was working for 12 hours a day and 6 days a week for 30p a week. In the same year a young laundress, Norah Higgs, sued her employer for back wages in a London county court. When the judge asked her how much she earned and how long she worked she replied 'Fourteen hours a day from 8 in the morning to 9 or 10 at night during which time I am not allowed to leave the works'. For this she was paid 50p a week.

The old, who were unable to work, were even worse off than the young and fit who could always hope that some work for some money might come their way as they wandered around the crowded streets of the industrial towns. The old, the sick and physically disabled were the least fortunate members of society.

The life style of the lowly paid

Jack London, an American reporter, wanted to find out something about the living conditions of the great mass of the British workers. He went to live among them and described his experiences in a novel *The People of the Abyss*, which graphically describes the poverty, dirt, smelly clothes, stinking and overcrowded rooms and the poor diet that these people had to put up with.

Charles Booth was a successful Liverpool shipping merchant who had made a fortune out of the growing trade of industrialised Britain. He read the propaganda put out by the various socialist societies (see Chapter 4) and refused to believe that this could be true. He set aside a vast sum of money to pay a team of enquirers who took 18 years to produce the 17 volumes *Life and Labour of the People in London*.

17 John Burns (third from right) at a meeting of the Finance Committee at the London Dockers' Strike Headquarters, the Wade Arms in Jeremiah Street, Poplar. This Committee was responsible for collecting funds, issuing food and other tickets to the strikers and their families. Their success encouraged unskilled workingmen to believe that they too could organise and succeed in the industrial and political field

In the process of producing this mammoth work, Booth discovered that the socialist societies had, if anything, understated the case for the poor. He discovered the family whose total income was 17s 7d (88p). He wrote:

This family live . . . to the greatest extent from hand to mouth. Not only do they buy almost everything on credit from one shop, but if the weeks tested are a fair sample of the year, they every week put in and take out of pawn the same set of garments, on which the broker every time advances 16s [80p], charging the no doubt reasonable sum of 4d [1½p] for the accommodation. They buy nothing till actually needed. They go to their shop as an ordinary housewife to her canisters; twice a day they buy tea, or three times if they make it so often; in 35 days they made 72 purchases of tea, amounting in all to 5s 2¾d [26p], and all most carefully noted down; the 'pinch of tea' costs ¾d (no doubt this is ½ oz at 2s per lb). Of sugar there are 77 purchases in the same time.

Seebohm Rowntree, a successful chocolate manufacturer, read some of Booth's work which was concerned with the poor of London. Rowntree, whose factory and home was in York, refused to believe that Booth's findings could be typical of Britain as a whole, although they might be true of London. He set up a team of enquirers to visit every home in York and his work *Poverty: a study of town life* (1900) showed that life in York, a typical small manufacturing town, was just as bad as life in London. He wrote: 'It is seen thus that the wages paid for unskilled labour in York are insufficient to provide food, shelter, and clothing adequate to maintain a family of moderate size in a state of bare physical efficiency'. One of his conclusions was: 'We have been accustomed to look upon the poverty in London as exceptional, but when the rest of careful investigation shows that the proportion of poverty in London is practically equalled in what may be regarded as a typical provincial town, we are faced by the startling probability that from 25 to 30 per cent of the town populations of the United Kingdom are living in poverty.'

The poorly paid could afford only poor quality housing, as described in *The Bitter Cry of Outcast London* (1883) by the Rev Andrew Mearns:

You have to penetrate courts reeking with poisonous and malodorous gases arising from the accumulations of sewage and refuse scattered in all directions; courts, many of which the sun never penetrates, which are never visited by a breath of fresh air. You have to ascend rotten staircases. You have to grope your way along dark and filthy passages swarming with vermin. Then you may gain admittance to the dens in which these thousands of beings, who belong as much as you to that race for whom Christ died, herd together. Eight feet square—that is about the average size of many of these rooms. As to furniture— you may perchance discover a broken chair; the tottering relic of an old bedstead or the mere fragment of a table; but more commonly you will find rude

18 Children of the City, 1904. These bare-footed boys tried to earn a few coppers either by sweeping the street-crossing (hence the brush) or by selling matches (box at left hand). Their poverty is reflected in their clothes as well as their listless attitude. They were the products of an industrialised society which showed little concern for those who did not succeed in helping themselves

substitutes for these things in the shape of rough boards resting upon bricks, an old hamper or box turned upside down, or more frequently still, nothing but rubbish and rags.

Workers in revolt

The skilled workers and their social superiors did not believe that it was any part of their work to do much about the poor—apart from contributing to a charitable collection out of which soup or clothes could be distributed. But in the 1880s the workers, led by middle-class intellectuals, began to take a hand in their own destiny.

Annie Besant was a middle-class journalist who organised a trade union and a strike at the match factory owned by Bryant and Mays, where workers, mainly young girls, worked long hours for 2d [less than 1p] an hour in disgusting conditions which frequently led to their getting a disease known as 'phossy jaw' as a result of the phosphorus fumes eating away at the bones of the jaw.

Her success inspired Will Thorne, a member of the Socialist Democratic Federation, to organise a union for the labourers who shovelled the coal into the ovens at the London Gas Light Company's works. Thorne threatened to call a strike unless the employers agreed to cut the working day from 12 to 8 hours without any reduction in wages. He was successful.

But the success of these two ventures paled into insignificance beside the strike organised by Tom Mann, Ben Tillett and John Burns acting on behalf of the labourers in London's docks. As *The Times* reported: 'The casual dock labourer occupied one of the most despised categories of labour. Possessing neither skill nor physique, he was considered incapable of bettering his condition by combination as so many more favoured workmen have done'.

Tillett, however, was determined that something could be done. As *Reynold's Newspaper* reported on 18 August 1889:

STRIKE OF DOCK LABOURERS.

The labourers engaged at the East and West India Docks have turned out on strike for an advance of 1d per hour in their wages, bringing their pay up to 6d [2½p] per hour, which sum is already paid to wharf and riverside labourers. Mass meetings of the men have been held and addressed by Mr B. Tillett, the Secretary of the Dock Labourers' Union and a leading member of the Stevedores' Society. [The stevedores were the better-paid, trained men who loaded ships for export.] As the average work of a dock labourer only amounts to three hours daily, the men consider their claim very moderate. Negotiations are actually on foot with a view to bringing the dispute to an end and the general feeling is that the companies will grant the demands of the men, many thousands of whom are affected by the dispute.

The employers and public opinion assumed that this strike would be brought quickly to an end; the men had no money, no skills, and could expect no support from the mass of the skilled workers on the docks. However, as *Reynold's Newspaper* reported on 1 September 1889:

When the strike was first announced a fortnight ago, the number of men amounted to about 10,000. Soon the figures reached 100,000 and even more. The dockmen themselves had no organisation. Had they been left to fight the battle alone, the dream of the Brutal Norwood, the chief of the capitalist gang at the docks, would have been, it is very probable, realised, and the pinch of poverty have driven the men into surrendering. But the sympathy of the stevedores was awakened. They protested and joined the dockmen. The gallant example was immediately followed by other riverside employees—shore gangs, carmen, firemen, scalers, iron-workers, coalies, 'lumpers', biscuit-makers, and labourers of every description. As days passed the strike grew in intensity and breadth.

Within five weeks the employers had been forced to climb down. *The Times* reported on 16 September 1889:

19 Gladstone introducing the first Irish Home Rule Bill in the Commons, April 1886 (just after the unemployed demonstration shown in Picture 15). The Liberal Party, of which he was the leader, made no attempt to do anything for the lower-paid and less-fortunate members of society

General rejoicing will hail the announcement that the strike is a thing of the past. It is an announcement which has been deferred so long that people had almost ceased to expect it. Now that it has come it is hardly less welcome to those concerned than the news of the conclusion of peace after an exhausting war. How much longer the strike might have dragged on but for the gallant efforts of Cardinal Manning, the Lord Mayor and Mr Sidney Buxton, can only be conjectured . . . The strike will remain a most significant event in the relations between capital and labour. There is first the fact that the despised dock labourers, possessed of no special skill, industry, or strength, and in regard to the last two qualifications often singularly ill-equipped, have been able to combine—combinations hitherto having been considered a weapon only available for the skilled labourer.'

Effects of the victory

The Times was the first to proclaim that this was a significant victory. It encouraged workers in other industries and trades to form their own unions for unskilled workers. Unlike the small and select Amalgamated Society of Engineers with a

20 John Burns (with back to the artist) and Cardinal Manning (hands folded on the far end of the table) who dominated the Conciliation Conference called by the Lord Mayor of London

membership of about 50,000, the unskilled unions recruited over 100,000 each. Unlike the select unions, they charged only 1d per week in fees, since their members earned so little. They had no funds, or welfare benefit schemes to help their members.

The value of the dockers' victory was limited—the men who managed to get work would, in future, get a minimum of 2s [10p] a day for their guaranteed 4 hours work. But this was a ridiculously small wage and was itself small comfort to the thousands who would not get any work at all.

If the life styles of the unskilled were to change—if their housing, education, diet, medical attention and life in old age was to improve—the State would have to step in and provide a welfare service for these people. But neither the Tory nor the Liberal Parties showed any signs of realising that this was required. Lord Rosebery, leader of the Liberals after Gladstone's retirement in 1893, had an income of over £100,000 a year and shared his old leader's belief that taxation was an evil which should be abolished as soon as possible. If the State was to make welfare provisions for the poor then taxation would have to be increased. This ran contrary to the whole philosophy of the Victorian Liberals. The Tories had turned their back on the memory of their old leader, Disraeli, who had given the vote to the working man in 1867, had passed the first effective Public Health Act, and might have realised the need to change his Party's policy towards the poor. But, under the aristocratic Lord Salisbury, the Tory Party was more concerned with advancing the interests of Britain's merchants in Africa, Asia and elsewhere, rather than with the poor at home.

Since the established parties were unwilling to do anything for them, and since their own trade union activity could accomplish only a small change in their conditions, what would the workers do next?

4 Socialism and Workers' Politics in Late-Victorian Britain

The mid-1880s

Ben Tillett, Tom Mann, John Burns and the leaders of the new unions for unskilled workers had all been affected by the spread of socialist propaganda in the early 1880s. In 1883 Karl Marx died, just before the first English translation of his *Das Kapital* appeared. Although few people read this mammoth work, those who did produced their own potted versions of Marxism in pamphlets, newssheets and lectures to workingmen's associations, so that the socialist message, often very much watered down, spread to a wider audience. In 1884 over one thousand people took part in a memorial march to Marx's grave at Highgate, London—an indication of the extent of his influence.

In 1881 the Socialist Democratic Federation had been formed by a small group who accepted the leadership of the upper-class H. M. Hyndman, who had read Marx's works and accepted the need for a socialist-led revolution. In 1884 a group broke away from the Federation which under the leadership of William Morris, the artist, formed the Socialist League.

21 A *Punch* cartoon showing Disraeli, Conservative Prime Minister 1874–80, succeeding at the Congress of Berlin (1878) in gaining Cyprus for Britain. Like the Liberals, the Conservatives did little for the less well-off, being more concerned with foreign affairs and the growth of the British Empire

35

22 The Socialist League, Hammersmith Branch. William Morris is fourth from the right in the second row

In 1884 another small group was formed by Edward Pease, who called his group the Fabians, after the Roman general who had managed to defeat Hannibal without fighting any battles. The Fabians were a London-based group of intellectuals who included H. G. Wells, the novelist, Bernard Shaw, the playwright, and Sidney and Beatrice Webb. The Fabians believed that the production of pamphlets with evidence of social injustice would ultimately be enough to convince right-thinking people of the need for reform. They hoped to convince the leaders of the existing political parties of this need; indeed, their main hope lay in convincing the leaders of the Liberal Party. Shaw was a member of the St Pancras Liberal Association and most of the Fabians were friendly with the leading politicians of the traditional parties.

A major work of propaganda was produced in the early 1880s by an American, Henry George, whose best-selling book was entitled *Progress and Poverty*. In this he demonstrated that governments could quite easily end the terrible conditions in which many people were living. What was required was a series of laws about housing, education, welfare benefits for the sick, old, unemployed and other unfortunate people, plus a system of taxation of the rich to provide the money to finance these reforms. This easily-read and popular book did a great deal to spread the socialist idea in the 1880s and 1890s. It was, however, only one of a series of best-selling books which appeared in the 1880s to stir the social conscience of the ruling class: Mearn's *The Bitter Cry of Outcast London*, the Salvation Army's *Darkest England*, along with Booth's massive work, which had a third edition in 1891, all sold widely.

The working class could neither afford to buy books such as this, nor did many of them have the time to read long works like Booth's. However, an ex-army sergeant, Robert Blatchford, living in Manchester, founded the *Clarion* in 1891. Not since the days of Cobbett's *Political Register* had a radical newspaper enjoyed such popularity. A penny edition of his *Merrie England* sold a million copies in 1894–95 and was a reprint of articles in the *Clarion*. Typical of his work was this extract from *Merrie England*:

Go out into the streets of any big English town, and use your eyes, John. What do you find? You find some rich and idle, wasting unearned wealth to their own shame and injury and the shame and injury of others. You find hard-working people packed away in vile, unhealthy streets. You find little children famished, dirty and half naked outside the luxurious clubs, shops, hotels and theatres. You find men and women overworked and underpaid. You find want and disease cheek by jowl with religion and culture and wealth. You find the usurer, the gambler, the fop, the finnikin fine lady, and you find the starveling, the slave, the drunkard, and the harlot. Is it nothing to you, John Smith?

Blatchford's readers formed themselves into *Clarion* cycling clubs, reading clubs, debating societies, choirs and other groups which drew together people who read and accepted the socialist ideas of this Manchester journalist.

James Keir Hardie
One of those who was affected by this stress of socialism was a Scottish miner, James Keir Hardie. Hardie was born in 1856, the illegitimate son of a farm servant. He went to work as a miner when he was eight years old, taught himself to read and write and by the age of fifteen was already involved in trade union work among

23 Robert Blatchford's *Clarion* was a popular means of spreading socialist propaganda

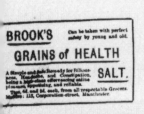

The CLARION

EDITED BY NUNQUAM.

BROOK'S GRAINS of HEALTH SALT. Can be taken with perfect safety by young and old. A Simple and Safe Remedy for Biliousness, Headache, and Constipation, being a refreshing effervescing saline pleasant, appetising, and reliable.

Try BURY'S SNOWDRIFT CAKE FLOUR. "IT'S A MARVEL. SOLD BY GROCERS EVERYWHERE.

No. 75. [REGISTERED FOR TRANSMISSION ABROAD.] SATURDAY, MAY 13, 1893. PRICE ONE PENNY.

ILD AND BITTER.

STRICTLY PROPER.
By Ed. Francis Jay.
[ALL RIGHTS RESERVED.]

the Scottish miners. He was a Liberal but when his local Association refused to adopt him as a Lib/Lab candidate he moved towards the idea of a separate political party for the working class. Upper-class landowners dominated the Tory Party, middle-class employers were represented by the Liberal Party; once the workers had been given the vote in 1867 it seemed logical that they should form their own party. This was the theme of his argument before the TUC conference in 1887 but the respectable working class refused to support him.

In 1888 Hardie fought the Mid-Lanark by-election as a miners' candidate but finished bottom of the poll. However, he went on to form the Scottish Labour Party in 1889, the first step along the long road to the formation of a national Labour Party. Hardie was only one leader among many: Tillett, Mann, Burns, Blatchford, Hyndman, Shaw—all of these and many others—claimed the right to speak for the working man. In 1893 Hardie managed to persuade these and other leaders to come to a conference at Bradford to discuss the formation of a workingmen's political party.

The conference was a success, Hardie and Tillett persuading their fellow delegates to adopt a practical programme. Tillett made clear that he 'wished to capture the trade unionists of this country, a body of men well organised, who paid their money and were socialists at their work every day and not merely on the platform'. The emphasis in the programme which the conference adopted was on practical objectives—the eight-hour day, provision for sickness and old age, free education and the abolition of indirect taxation.

Following this conference Bernard Shaw wrote a letter to trade unionists throughout the country, appealing to them to support this new Party, which in the 1895 election put forward 28 candidates, none of whom was elected. However, the trade union movement was still dominated by the leaders of the skilled unions with their Lib/Lab ambitions, their acceptance of the Liberal ideas of self-help and their acceptance also of the social system which had done them a great deal of good. They wanted nothing to do with this socialist appeal to the masses.

John Burns attended the TUC conferences in the 1880s, and wrote: 'The leaders of the craft unions looked exactly like the employers in their heavy overcoats, dark suits and heavy watch chains. Only the delegates of the unskilled unions looked like workers.'

But the nature of the conference was due to change in the 1890s. First, there was an ever-increasing number of delegates from the constantly growing unions for unskilled workers. These, in the main, were socialist in outlook and readily supported Hardie's annual appeal for TUC support for the Independent Labour Party. In the course of the 1890s the nature of the delegates representing the skilled unions also changed. Some, like George Barnes of the Engineers' Union, were members of socialist societies who managed to convince their own delegates to support Hardie's appeals. Others, although suspicious of the unskilled unions' demands, became less certain of their own position and of the virtues of free

24 Keir Hardie (left) with George Bernard Shaw (right) and Shaw's wife. Shaw, a popular playwright, was a member of the Fabian Society. It was his letter to the TUC which led that organisation to support Hardie's call for a Labour Party—in which the Fabian Society played a major role

This is to Certify that

J Keir Hardie M.P.

is a member of the

National Independent Labour Party

for the year 1895.

25 Keir Hardie was a founder member of the ILP. This is his membership card for 1895, when Tom Mann —the Dockers' leader— was Secretary and Hardie was President

enterprise when, during the 1890s, their members suffered heavy and long-term unemployment. Their welfare funds had been designed to help members to cope with short–term and temporary unemployment. But the development of German and American industry led to a decline in the level of British exports and a consequent falling-off in employment prospects for millions of British workers. Liberalism and Toryism had nothing to offer these skilled men who now joined the ranks of the poor. Their fellow unionists, fearing that this might be their fate, began to listen to socialist propaganda.

The birth of the Labour Party

In 1899 the delegates from the Railway Servants' Union (now the NUR) put forward the resolution:

> To invite the co-operation of all the co-operative, socialistic, trade union, and other working organizations to jointly co-operate on lines mutually agreed upon, in convening a social congress of representatives from such above named organisations as may be willing to take part to devise ways and means for securing the return of an increased number of Labour members to the next Parliament.

26 Part of *The Times* report of the meeting at the Memorial Hall, Farringdon Street, London in 1900, when representatives of some trade unions, the Fabian Society, the Social Democratic Federation, and Hardie's Independent Labour Party formed the Labour Representation Committee which, in 1906, changed its name to the Labour Party. Notice the speech by John Burns—who later joined the Liberal Party—and that by MacDonald who first became Secretary of the new Committee and later became Labour's first Prime Minister

Mr. JONES (representing Upholsterers) moved—"That this conference is in favour of the working-class opinion being represented in the House of Commons by members of the working classes, as being the most likely to be sympathetic with the aims and demands of the labour movement."

Mr. PAUL VOGEL (Waiters' Union) seconded.

Mr. GEORGE BARNES moved an amendment in favour of working-class opinion being represented " by men sympathetic with the aims of the labour movement, and whose candidatures are promoted by one or other of the organized movements represented at the conference."

Mr. JOHN BURNS, M.P., in seconding the amendment, said the resolution was narrow, intolerant, and exclusive. He was, he said, getting rather tired of hearing about workmen's boots, workmen's trains, workmen's dwellings, workmen's clothes, and working men candidates for working-class colonies. (Hear, hear.) The time had arrived in the history of the labour movement when they should no longer allow themselves to be prisoners to class phrases. (Laughter and " Hear, hear.") Did they propose to select boiler makers who earned £3 or £4 a week and reject clerks who dressed like dukes on the wages of dustmen ? (Laughter.) A navvy might be elected a Parliamentary representative, and if he became a great contractor would they reject him ?

The amendment was carried by 102 votes against 3.

The Parliamentary Committee submitted a resolution " in favour of establishing a distinct labour group in Parliament, who should have their own Whips and agree upon their policy, which must embrace a readiness to co-operate with any party which for the time being may be engaged in promoting legislation in the direct interest of labour, and be equally ready to associate themselves with any party in opposing measures having an opposite tendency," but in its place

Mr. JAMES MACDONALD moved—" The representatives of the working-class movement in the House of Commons shall form there a distinct party, with a party organization entirely separate from the capitalist parties, based upon a recognition of the class war, and having for its ultimate object the socialization of the means of production, distribution, and exchange : the party shall formulate its own policy for promoting practical legislative measures in the interests of labour, and shall be prepared to co-operate with any party that will support such measures or will assist in opposing measures of an opposite character."

When this was put to the vote it was approved by 546,000 to 434,000—many leaders of skilled unions still throwing their weight, and their members' votes, against the resolution. On 27 February 1900, delegates met at the Memorial Hall in Farringdon Street, London, and this may be regarded as the birthplace of the Labour Party. One hundred and twenty-nine trade union delegates attended; seven led by Hardie, with the young Ramsay MacDonald represented the ILP, four came from the SDF and one from the Fabians. The remainder were trade unionists—although they represented less than half of the 1,205,000 members affiliated to the TUC.

The conference revealed the split between the socialist-minded and those who wanted to work out a more practical, less dogmatic policy. As Philip Snowden, later Labour Chancellor of the Exchequer, recalled:

An attempt was made by the Social Democrats to commit the conference to a declaration that the new Party should be based on the recognition of the class war, with socialism as its ultimate aim. This was an illustration of the tactlessness of the Social Democrats, which explained the reason for the failure of their propaganda to make any impression on public opinion. At this stage to commit the trade unions to an extreme socialist programme would have made the co-operation of the bodies represented at the conference impossible. Keir Hardie, with a true appreciation of the situation, and of the importance of carrying the trade unions by stages to the ultimate goal, moved on behalf of the ILP an amendment . . .

'That this Conference declares in favour of establishing a distinct Labour group in Parliament, who should have their own whips and agree upon their policy, which must embrace a readiness to co-operate with any party which for the time being may be engaged in promoting legislation in the direct interest of Labour, and be equally ready to associate themselves with any party in opposing measures having an opposite tendency'.

(*From 'An Autobiography' by Viscount Philip Snowden, published 1934 by Ivor Nicholson and Watson.*)

The significance of the alliance between the unions and the smaller socialist societies was revealed when J. Hodge (Manchester) moved 'That the Executive Committe shall consist of 12 representatives, seven of whom shall represent the trade unions, one the Fabian Society, two the ILP and two the SDF. Such members shall be elected by their respective organisations'.

This domination by trade unionists was seen to be fair when another resolution was carried which said 'That the Committee shall administer the funds which may be received on behalf of the organisation and each body shall be required to pay 10s [50p] per annum for every 1,000 members or fraction thereof; also that they shall be responsible for the expenses of their own candidates'. Obviously the trade unions, with their larger membership, were going to pay the piper; by controlling the Executive Committee they were also going to call the tune, although only 40 out of 1,200 trade unions did affiliate to the Labour Representation Committee.

Each of the separate groups was to be responsible for financing the election expenses of their candidates—the trade unions would put forward their candidates, the ILP its own candidates and so on. There was as yet no national Labour Party organisation; the Committee was merely a federation of existing societies. No one could join the Labour Party as such—a man could join a union affiliated to the Committee or could join the Fabian Society or the ILP and thus become a member and supporter of the LRC.

In 1900 fifteen LRC candidates took part in the general election and while each was separately financed the LRC itself spent £33 on the election. Only two candidates were successful—Hardie won at Merthyr in South Wales and Richard Bell of the Railway Servants' Union won at Derby, the home of much of the railway engineering industry. In addition, there were 8 Liberal trade unions MPs (Lib/Labs). This was the small beginning from which the Labour Party was to grow in the course of the twentieth century.

27 John Burns speaking at Derby in support of Richard Bell (seated, left) at the 1906 election. Bell had been one of the two ILP MPs in 1900, but like many of his fellow skilled workers, he was never at home in the Labour Party, which he left to become a Liberal candidate. Burns, who had once condemned the skilled workers' delegates at TUC conferences had now become 'respectable' and even joined the Liberal government; they were not the last ones to discover that nothing succeeds like secession

5 The First Years of the Labour Party, 1900—1914

More trade unions join

In August 1900, after the Memorial Hall meeting but before the general election, railway workers on the Taff Vale Railway in South Wales went on a strike which, after some time, their Union recognised and made official. The strike was a failure but the Company decided to prosecute the Amalgamated Society of Railway Servants for damages caused to company property during this strike. No one expected the Company to win but in July 1901 the House of Lords awarded £23,000 damages to the Company and also ordered the Union to pay £19,000 in legal costs. This was an indication of the growing hostility towards trade unionism.

28 A poster issued by the Amalgamated Society of Railway Servants, later known as the National Union of Railwaymen, during the Taff Vale Railway Strike, Strike, 1900. Richard Bell was already an MP

STRIKE !
ON THE
Taff Vale Railway.

Men's Headquarters,
Cobourn Street,
Cathays.

There has been a strike on the Taff Vale Railway since Monday last. The Management are using every means to decoy men here who they employ for the purpose of black-legging the men on strike.

Drivers, Firemen, Guards, Brakesmen, and
SIGNALMEN, are all out.

Are you willing to be known as a
Blackleg ?

If you accept employment on the Taff Vale, that is what you will be known by. On arriving at Cardiff, call at the above address, where you can get information and assistance.

RICHARD BELL,
General Secretary.

43

The Tory government, led by A. J. Balfour, could have set trade union fears at rest by passing simple legislation. Since the government refused to act, an increasing number of trade union leaders began to see that they needed a voice in the Commons to speak for them. As Arthur Henderson said in 1903:

> The adverse decision of the Law Courts, which has endangered the accumulated investments of trade unions, the aggregation of capital by the formation of huge trusts, the high pressure of modern industry, and its effects on employment, the terrific problems of slumdom—these and many other reasons can be advanced why we should see that Labour, which constitutes three-fourths of the forty-two million people in this country, is more adequately represented, and in such a way that its first consideration will always be to do that which will promote the common weal.

Many of the unions which had stood apart from the meeting which led to the formation of the LRC now saw the need to join. At the Annual Conference of the LRC in 1903, 'Mr Hodge said the progress of their movement was shown by the fact that when they met last year, at Birmingham, the numbers affiliated to the LRC were 456,531, and today the numbers were 751,570, an increase of more

29 The cheque made out to the Taff Vale Railway Company as settlement for the Company's claims against the ASRS. The General Secretary of the Society was Richard Bell (bottom left hand), a founder member of the Labour Party

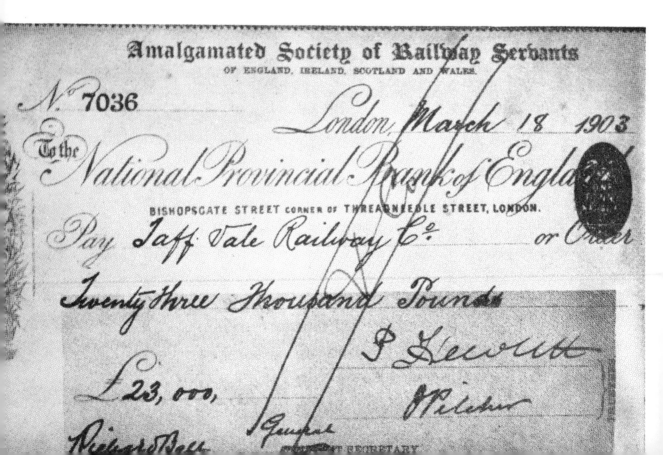

30 Arthur Henderson addressing a trade union meeting in Dublin, 1913. Henderson and many of his workmates became politically conscious not through any formal education but by their involvement in the unions and from reading material issued by Hardie, the ILP, the Fabian Society, and Blatchford's *Clarion*

than 300,000. During the last few weeks the textile workers had come in, making the figures more like 852,000 an increase of about 100 per cent'.

These new recruits from the older, skilled unions brought to the infant Party not only large numbers, but also great experience in negotiating, ability in organising and the framework through their branches of a national organisation around which the new Party could grow.

Liberals make an alliance, 1903

In 1903 the LRC imposed a levy on all its members to provide 25 per cent of the expenses of all candidates and a salary of £200 a year for MPs. In this way the Committee hoped to gain control over the LRC members. After successful by-elections, Hardie and Bell were joined by David Shackleton from the Weavers' Union, who was elected for Clitheroe, Will Crooks of the Coopers', elected for Woolwich, and Arthur Henderson of the Ironfounders', elected for Barnard Castle.

But these by-election successes showed that the LRC candidates did well only in areas where the Liberals withdrew their candidates or where the Liberal candidate fared badly. With the general election looming ahead, the LRC leaders realised that they would do badly if their candidates had to fight against

31 Labour MPs on the Terrace of the House of Commons, 1911. Hardie is seated third from the right; behind him is Philip Snowden, a future Chancellor of the Exchequer; standing in the second row, centre, is Ramsay MacDonald, Labour's first Prime Minister in 1924

both Tory and Liberal candidates. The Liberals, on the other hand, were not confident that they could win enough seats to overturn the Tory majority. Herbert Gladstone, the Liberal Chief Whip, held a series of secret meetings with Ramsay MacDonald as a result of which both the anti-Tory parties agreed to persuade some of their local associations to withdraw candidates to allow only one of the anti-Tories a free run. This electoral pact was a great success for the LRC, which put 50 candidates into the field and found that 29 of them won seats. Of these, 22 represented trade unions and 7 came from the ILP. In addition, there were 13 miners' MPs, 4 MPs put forward by trade unions not affiliated to the Labour Party (as the LRC was named after 1906), and 7 other Lib/Lab workingmen's MPs. Labour was represented by 53 MPs in the 1906 Parliament. Even though the Liberals won a massive victory over the Tories, A. J. Balfour—looking at the body of Labour MPs—remarked that this was the really important feature of the election result. In the long run he was correct.

In Parliament, 1906–14
The Labour MPs saw themselves, first of all, as a pressure group representing the interests of the trade unions who paid their salaries. In 1906 they persuaded the Liberal government to pass the Trades Disputes Act which set aside the Taff Vale judgment. They also, in general, supported the Liberals' introduction of some welfare legislation—the first Old Age Pensions Act, the National Insurance Act, 1911 and the Parliament Act, 1911 which truncated the power of the House of Lords. But the more socialist–minded—both inside and outside Parliament—were

46

The Industrial
MONTHLY Syndicalist

Vol. I., No. 4.   ONE PENNY.   Oct., 1910.

SUBSCRIPTION.
Great Britain or Abroad ... 12 Months, 1s.6d.

All Hail,
Industrial Solidarity!

BRAVO! BRAVO! COMRADES OF FRANCE!

By the announcement in No. 3 of the "Industrial Syndicalist," readers would be expecting No. 4 to deal chiefly with the Reduction of Working Hours; the same was written and sent to press, but when the French Industrial struggle assumed such proportions it was decided to reserve the matter for another occasion. In the meantime, it is necessary to say that for various reasons there is no subject of equal importance to that of Reducing the Hours of Working.

Whilst the unemployed exist in the numbers they now do, the workers

32 Tom Mann had led the Dockers' Strike in 1889. By 1910 he had become a convert to syndicalism, an international movement which wanted workers' control of the industries in which they worked—the miners should control the coal industry, the dockers should take over the docks and so on. The formation of large unions in the early part of this century seemed to many people to be the one step along the road to syndicalist control; many people thought that the General Strike of 1926 was a last fling by the syndicalists

not content with this infant Welfare State. It did little for the poor, the unemployed or the sick and, in any case, the cost of most of these changes was to be paid by the working men and not by the richer taxpayer. The socialists in the Labour Party wanted more than this. Labour Party activists outside Parliament failed to see that an independent party had made much contribution towards change; the social revolution seemed as far away as ever.

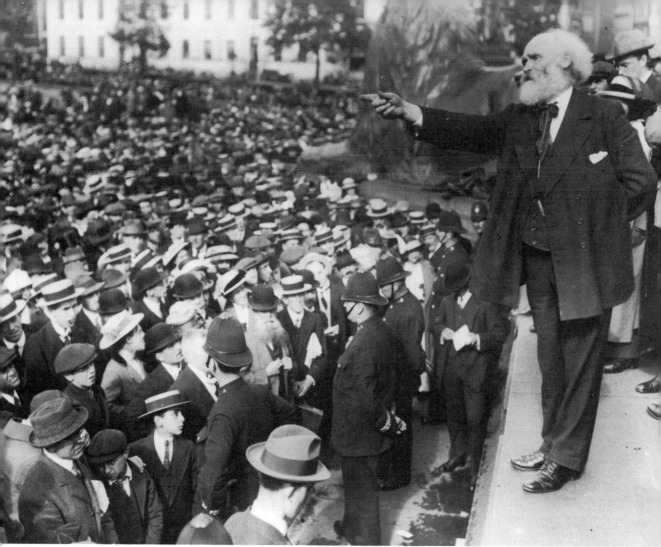

33 Keir Hardie addressing an anti-war demonstration in Trafalgar Square, August 1914. This pacifism split the Party and made it very unpopular for the time being

Between 1910–14 this discontent showed itself in a number of ways. The Party fought 14 by-elections without winning one, while 4 Labour-held seats were lost in the elections of 1910. Party support was obviously lukewarm. Working-class supporters of socialism tended to believe that the politicians would not change anything—or would change it too slowly. Some began to preach a new doctrine of syndicalism which taught that the workers in an industry should take control of that industry and run it for their own benefit and not for the benefit of the profit-making owners. This doctrine was popular with the miners, who invited the railway workers and transport workers to join them in a Triple Alliance which would, they claimed, be able to force employer and government to adopt policies more favourable to Labour. This doctrine was to lead to the General Strike of 1926 (Chapter 7).

Militancy

The period of 1910–14 was one of unprecedented social unrest. Militant women suffragettes captured the headlines with their campaign. In Ireland the Ulster Protestants, with the active support of the Tory Party, were planning a civil war against the Liberal government's 'Home Rule for Ireland' Bill, which was due to come into operation in 1914. In England the Lords, by throwing out the Budget in 1909, started off a constitutional crisis which involved the country in two general elections in 1910 and led to the passing of the Parliament Act in 1911.

In the middle of this unrest there was the growth of a new kind of trade union militancy. There had been strikes in the past and these had often led to violent clashes between strikers and blacklegs brought in by employers with the support of the police. But in 1911 and 1912 the country saw the first of the national strikes called by the now very large (over 300,000 members) Transport Workers' Union and by the equally large Railway Workers' Union.

Labour organisation

But if some extremists hoped to change the world by activities outside Parliament, the Labour Party made preparations for a slower, if more definite, change in the nation's life. By 1914 there were local Labour organisations of one sort or another in 158 areas, while the ILP had 672 branches. Strength was greatest in the north

34 The British Labour Party welcomed the Russian Revolution which overthrew the Tsarist regime. Will Thorne, the former Dockers' leader, (seated, centre) led a Labour Party Delegation to Russia in April, before Lenin and the Bolsheviks overthrew the government

49

of England, London, Scotland and South Wales. In 1911 Ramsay MacDonald became Chairman of the Labour Party in succession to Hardie, and Henderson succeeded MacDonald as Secretary of the Labour Party. Henderson had a good local Labour organisation in his own constituency of Barnard Castle, and he built up an equally effective national organisation.

The war, 1914

All this was thrown into doubt when Britain declared war on Germany in August 1914. The Party's election manifesto in 1906 had declared that 'wars are fought to make the rich richer'. Contact with socialists from France, Germany, Russia, Belgium and other countries only convinced the leaders of the Labour Party that war was a capitalist trick, that the workers stood to gain nothing from it and that combined action by the workers of the world would mean that no country could declare war on another since workers and soldiers would not fight.

On 2 August, 1914 Hardie addressed an anti-war rally in Trafalgar Square, in which he declared that an 'international strike would make war impossible'. But when Germany invaded Belgium the mood of the Party and its supporters changed. Hardie was shouted down in his own constituency; the Party agreed not to oppose the Liberal government's war Budget. MacDonald, still an anti-war pacifist, resigned and Henderson, who had shared the Trafalgar Square platform with Hardie, became the leader of the Parliamentary Party. Throughout the country Fabians, trade unionists and other supporters became flag-waving patriots. Only a section of the small ILP remained opposed to the war right to the end and they were joined in their pacifism by some radical Liberals who later joined the Labour Party.

The party in government

But the war had its benefits for the Party. In May, 1915, Asquith invited Henderson to enter his Coalition Cabinet. In 1916 a similar invitation went to Hodge who became Minister of Labour, and to Barnes who became Minister of Pensions when Lloyd George became Prime Minister. Throughout the country the government set up hundreds of committees and advisory councils all of which aimed at ironing out one problem or another which hindered the war effort. This experience gained by trade union branch secretaries and shop stewards gave them a taste for power.

With more people at work than ever before, the individual trade unions became larger and wealthier while their leaders became more experienced and ambitious. The working men and their families enjoyed a higher standard of living in wartime than most of them had had in the 'golden age' of Edwardian England. Many were now able to buy meat and fresh fruit, to buy new and not secondhand clothes and thousands of children enjoyed the pleasure of wearing shoes for the first time.

Ernest Bevin, a trade union leader, complained that working people suffered from 'a poverty of desire'—meaning that they had a very poor idea of what they wanted out of life. But during wartime many of them experienced a new standard of living and learned to desire better and more goods. This led them to have greater expectations from life than they might otherwise have had. One result of this was, in the long term, an increased support for the Labour Party which appeared to be the only party which could produce a programme destined to satisfy these desires.

The Liberals and the war

Perhaps the greatest benefit that the war brought to the Labour Party was that it split the Liberal Party between those who followed Lloyd George in his rebellion against Asquith in 1916 and those who remained faithful to Asquith. By 1918 this split had created such hostility between former colleagues in the Liberal Party that they opposed each other on platforms with greater vigour than they opposed either the Tory or Labour candidates. One effect of this was to create a vacuum on the left wing of politics; the Tory Party occupied the right wing; the Liberal Party had occupied the left wing with some support from the infant Labour Party. With the split in the Liberal Party many anti-Tories now voted Labour—not so much out of support for Labour as such, but out of anti-Toryism which had previously been expressed in a vote for the now split Liberals.

A new constitution

Henderson and Sidney Webb realised that the Labour Party suffered as a result of its being a federation of local societies. Together, they wrote a new constitution for the Party which was adopted by a Party Conference in February 1918. The new constitution set out the object of the Party as being to 'secure for the producers by hand and by brain the full fruits of their industry and the most equitable distribution thereof that may be possible, upon the basis of the common ownership of the means of production, and the best obtainable system of popular administration and control of each industry and service'.

There was also an attempt to widen the basis of Party membership. In the past, non-manual workers could only become members of the Party by joining one or other of the socialist societies. But their combined membership was never more than 75,000. Obviously, they did not make an appeal to the mass of the non-manual workers. Labour needed to recruit support if it was to win power. Nor was there much room in these societies for the six million women who were given the vote in 1918. Henderson and Webb established a new national Party organisation, setting up local Labour Party Associations to recruit individuals 'who subscribe to the constitution and programme of the Party'. Five of the twenty-three members of the enlarged National Executive Committee were to represent these local Labour Parties and four other places were reserved for representatives of women's organisations.

Labour and the new social order

By 1918 the membership of the Party had risen to three million, reflecting the growth in trade union membership. Because of the 1918 Reform Act there were now over twenty-one million voters, compared to the eight million who had been allowed to vote in 1910. To appeal to this new electorate the Labour Party leaders produced a full programme of policies in an historic document, *Labour and the New Social Order*, which was approved by the Party Conference in June 1918. This stated the need to 'build a new social order based, not on internecine conflict, inequality of riches and dominion over subject classes . . . but on the deliberately planned co-operation in production and distribution . . . the widest possible participation in power, both economic and political, and the general consciousness of concert which characterises a true democracy'.

It set out a detailed programme for the nationalisation of land and certain basic industries, the planning of the economy, the maintenance of full employment and the provision of adequate welfare and social security. These formed the basis of Labour's programme for the next twenty-five years and of the policies carried out by the Labour government after 1945 (Chapter 8).

The Party in 1918

At first the war had threatened to split the Labour Party as it was to split the Liberals. But in the long run the war proved to be a beneficial influence for the Labour Party. It became a national Party, capable of governing the country; it grew in numbers; it had defined its policies and explained its objectives. It could face the future with more confidence than had seemed possible in the uncertain days of 1914.

6   The Party of Protest becomes the Party of Government, 1918-1925

Boom and slump

In the immediate post-war period the greater expectations of the working class seemed about to be fulfilled. Employment levels were at a record height as the country made up for the four years of war during which there had been little domestic development. Rebuilding, modernisation and new development led to more workers finding jobs and employers being willing to offer higher wages.

In this situation the more confident and ambitious trade union movement flourished. The railwaymen, led by J. H. Thomas, the transport workers led by Ernest Bevin and the miners led by Frank Smith, forced employers to concede high wage rates. Everything seemed to be for the best in the best of all possible worlds.

But in 1921 this apparent Utopia came to a sudden end. There was growing competition from the USA, Germany, Japan and other countries, while many former customers such as India, had developed their own industries. British exports slumped—and as they did so unemployment levels rose and in 1922 over 11 per cent were out of work.

Politics in boom and slump

In 1918 Lloyd George had led his wartime Coalition into an election in which he asked the enlarged electorate to give him the majority he required to 'win the peace'. Sir Roy Harrod remembered the election:

> The general election of 1918 involved a vulgarisation of British public life . . . With the enlarged electorate, a fluid social and economic system and, it must be added, with the women—on whom party doctrine did not have so strong a hold—receiving the vote, there were growing numbers of the electors whose politics were not based on well-defined doctrines. It was these who were the ready prey of the vulgarisers in political journalism and, finally, in political leadership . . . Lacking settled principles, such slogans as 'Hang the Kaiser', or 'Squeeze the lemon until the pips squeak' gave them convenient matter for private oratory. . . . In this vulgarisation Lloyd George played his part . . . Thus he collected his Parliament of what Mr Baldwin called 'hard-faced men who look as if they have done very well out of the war'. (*From 'The Life of J. M. Keynes' by Sir Roy Harrod, published 1951 by Macmillan.*)

It may have been vulgar, but from Lloyd George's point of view it was very

YESTERDAY - THE TRENCHES

35 These two election posters reflect the sense of hopelessness felt by many millions of people; they had been promised a country 'fit for heroes to live in'; in fact, there were always over one million and often over two million unemployed in the 1920s

TO-DAY—UNEMPLOYED

successful. His supporters won 478 seats (338 being won by Conservatives, who were willing to follow Lloyd George for the time being). Asquith's supporters won only 26 seats so that the Labour Party, with 57 seats, became for the first time the official Opposition. Writing about this new Parliament, Lloyd George remembered that it was a 'curious assembly, . . . quite different . . . from any other House of Commons I have known. When I was speaking I felt, as I looked in front of me, that I was addressing a Trade Union Congress. Then, when I turned around, I felt as if I were speaking to a Chamber of Commerce'.

The Labour success was marred by the failure of so many of the leaders to get elected. Among those who failed were Henderson, MacDonald, Snowden, Jowett, Lansbury, Bevin and Sidney Webb. Of those elected, 25 had been put forward by the Miners' Federation, 24 by other trade unions and only 3 had been nominated by the ILP.

Perhaps the most significant feature of the election was that for the first time the Labour Party fought without the benefit of a pact with the Liberals, faced opposition from the candidates put forward by the Liberals and by the Coalition government, and yet succeeded in winning 59 seats. The Party had received two and a quarter million votes—about one-quarter of all the votes cast.

Lloyd George's fall

By 1922 Lloyd George's government had become unpopular; it had failed to deal with the problem of unemployment, it had not built a country 'fit for heroes to live in' as he had promised in 1918, the leader had quarrelled with Dominion countries over the possibility of making war on Turkey and had annoyed many of his parliamentary supporters by his increasingly dictatorial manner. The majority of these supporters were Tories and although their leaders—members of the Cabinet—were unwilling to challenge Lloyd George, the Tory 'second eleven' led by Stanley Baldwin, a junior Minister at the Treasury, asked that the Tory Party should leave the Coalition and fight the next election as an independent party.

When this motion was put to a vote of all Tory MPs at a meeting at the Carlton Club in London on 19 October, 1922, to many people's surprise, the second eleven won. Although most Tory leaders continued to support Lloyd George, the mass of Tory MPs followed Bonar Law and Baldwin in deciding to leave the Coalition. Lloyd George was forced to resign and a general election was called in 1922. Bonar Law and the Conservatives won 347 seats, Labour won 142 seats, while the Liberals—divided in their loyalty to Lloyd George and Asquith—could win only 117 seats. The Labour vote rose to four and a quarter million which was about one-third of all the votes cast. All the leaders were returned except Henderson. Among the outstanding newcomers to Parliament were Clement Attlee, Sidney Webb, Arthur Greenwood and a group of very left-wing and militant Clydesiders of whom James Maxton, David Kirkwood and Emanuel Shinwell were the most outstanding. Shinwell, on behalf of the Clydesiders, nominated Ramsay MacDonald as the Party's leader—although he had been defeated in 1918 after a wartime record as a pacifist. The handsome and eloquent Scot beat J. R. Clynes, leader since 1918, by 61 votes to 56 and by these five votes the Party decided who was soon to be Labour's first Prime Minister.

36 The Countess of Warwick was a Labour supporter and often entertained Labour leaders at her home at Easton Lodge. In this picture taken in 1923, are (from left to right) *standing:* Otto Wells, Canon Adderley, Mr and Mrs Shinwell and Will Thorne, *seated:* Arthur Henderson, the Countess, Ramsay MacDonald and Rudolf Breitscheid. Shinwell and MacDonald were to meet in less favourable surroundings in 1935.

Baldwin and tariffs

Baldwin succeeded Bonar Law as Prime Minister in 1923 and announced that while he believed that a possible cure of unemployment was the introduction of a system of tariffs, he also realised that this was a major step, since it meant the end of Free Trade on which Britain's greatness had been built in the nineteenth century. He decided to call a general election to ask for the nation's support for this policy. However, the Tories won only 258 seats (a loss of 87) while the Labour Party won 191 (a gain of 49) and the two wings of the Liberal Party won 158 seats (a gain of 42). Early in January 1924 the Labour and Liberal Parties united to defeat Baldwin's government in the Commons and Baldwin resigned.

MacDonald and office

Baldwin advised King George V to send for MacDonald as the leader of the second largest party in the Commons, to ask him to try to form a government. Many Tories thought that this was a mistake; they wanted Baldwin to make an alliance with the Liberals to keep MacDonald out, or to call another election to give the British people a chance to vote against this threat of government by the Labour 'bogeymen'.

Baldwin realised that if he did either of these things the Labour Party would have just cause to complain that the rules of the parliamentary game were rigged against them. If they did this, some of their wilder supporters might take matters into their own hands and try to seize power by force, as Lenin and the Bolsheviks had recently done in Russia. In any case the British electorate would not be hoodwinked like this. As Baldwin knew, one of the main appeals of the Labour Party was its idealism, its apparent moral approach to the nation's problems, which made a stark contrast with the cynical way in which Lloyd George had governed. If the Tories tried to keep the Labour Party out the electorate would regard this, cynically, as yet another example of the dishonesty of the traditional politicians as opposed to the idealism of the new Labour Party.

Baldwin also realised that if MacDonald and his Party did turn out to be extremists (an unlikely prospect), it would be a simple matter for the combined Tory and Liberal Parties to drive them out of power. While Baldwin thought that MacDonald and the Labour Party should be allowed to have their share of power, he also realised that it would be power being exercised under great constraint.

Many of MacDonald's supporters realised this. They thought that MacDonald should refuse to take office since he would have to depend on Liberal support if he wanted to get anything done. He would, in fact, be a prisoner of the traditional parties and socialism would not be given a fair chance.

It was MacDonald's own opinion that he ought to accept the King's invitation and try to form a government even though his freedom would be hedged around because of his lack of a majority. MacDonald thought that it was important to show the country as a whole and the Party's supporters in particular that working-class men from industrial employment could run Cabinet Offices and govern the country. He believed that this would by psychologically good for the Party and it would also be of great practical value—since a hundred or so Labour MPs would have to become actively involved in running the country as members of the government. This experience would stand them in good stead when, in the future, the Party gained an overall majority.

37 The first Labour government, 1924—not the stuff of which Lenin-type revolutions were made. This picture, taken in the garden of Number 10 Downing Street, is a memorial of Labour's entry into the corridors of power

And so on 22 January 1924 MacDonald, Henderson and Clynes went to Buckingham Palace to accept the King's invitation to form a government. It was indeed a great change in the country's political life. As Clynes wrote in his *Memoirs*:

King George sent for Mr MacDonald. Arthur Henderson, J. H. Thomas and myself accompanied our leader to Buckingham Palace, to that fateful interview of which we had dreamed, when a British Sovereign should entrust the affairs of his Empire to the hands of the people's own representatives.

As we stood waiting for His Majesty, amid the gold and crimson magnificence of the Palace, I could not help marvelling at the strange turn of Fortune's wheel, which had brought MacDonald, the starveling clerk, Thomas the engine-driver, Henderson, the foundry labourer and Clynes, the mill-hand, to this pinnacle beside the man whose forebears had been kings for so many splendid generations. We were making history.

British voting habits
MacDonald's insistence on forming a government was based on the idea that this would draw increasing attention to the Party and make it more likely that more people would vote for it in the future. We know now that about 80 per cent of people vote in the way in which their parents voted, and about 90 per cent of us vote throughout our lives for the party which we supported when we voted for the first time. This meant that the older parties—Tory and Liberal—had a built-in advantage in the Labour Party's early days, since the voting habits of the electorate had been established when there were only two parties to vote for. But as an increasing number of people began to vote Labour, and as Labour replaced the Liberals as the natural alternative to the Tory Party, this built-in tendency began to help the Labour Party. The Liberal Party continued to be supported by a dwindling number of older voters and some of their children, but an increasing number of younger voters were beginning to vote Labour—and in the future this would mean that their children would be likely to do so as well.

MacDonald's government
The government tried to deal with unemployment: benefits were increased and plans were announced for road and railway construction to provide jobs. John Wheatley, the Minister of Health, announced plans to provide subsidies to local councils which built houses to be let at controlled rents which the poor could afford. Charles Trevelyan set in motion some minor reforms in education which were to lead to the setting up of secondary modern schools in place of the all-age elementary schools.

In foreign affairs MacDonald persuaded the French to withdraw from the Ruhr; he supported Dawes's plan for reducing German reparations and he actively supported the League of Nations. In particular the Labour government recognised the Soviet government and planned to make a British loan to them. This was one of the reasons why the government became unpopular.

38 The 'Zinoviev letter' which seemed to many to be proof that the Labour Party and the trade union movement was under the control of the Russian Communist government. The letter was probably a forgery; certainly the Labour Party never came under Communist control

The fall of the government

The Attorney General, Sir Patrick Hastings, had initiated a prosecution against the editor of a Communist journal which had urged soldiers to refuse to take up arms against the working class either at home or abroad. In theory there was a case to be made against the Communist editor, J. R. Campbell, but it would have been a very tactless prosecution. Hastings decided to drop the prosecution, which led the Tories and Liberals to combine to defeat the government. MacDonald then decided to call a general election in October 1924, the third in three years.

The election

The 1924 election is best remembered for the affair of the Zinoviev letter which was supposed to have been sent from the Communist International to the British Communist Party urging it to prepare for a military revolution in Britain. This letter was published in the *Daily Mail* and was used by Labour's opponents to whip up a 'red scare' and the public became almost hysterical in its fear of a Bolshevik takeover. As G.M. Young wrote: 'The one thing certain . . . was that powerful elements of the Left had transferred their allegiance to a foreign power, which was working, not silently and secretly but loudly and ostentatiously for the subversion of English institutions'.

However, the Party increased its share of the poll—receiving over five and a half million votes. But this was offset by the fact that it won only 152 seats while the Tories won 415. One bright ray for the Labour Party—apart from the increase in its votes—was that the combined Liberal Parties won only 40 seats and became even less important. The future belonged to the Tory and Labour Parties.

7 Revolution or Evolution, 1925-1929?

The failure of the MacDonald government

While MacDonald and his fellow Ministers had indeed made history by forming the first Labour government, their supporters throughout the country had a right to feel disappointed with the results of this historic step. Unemployment was higher in 1925 than it had been when MacDonald became Prime Minister; the government had not tried to implement any of the socialist policies outlined in *Labour and the New Social Order*, and although unemployment benefit had been increased many people felt that this Labour government had only behaved like a radical Liberal government might have behaved.

The result of the general election of 1924 confirmed this popular belief that the traditional parties could always manipulate affairs to suit themselves. MacDonald and his colleagues were no more likely to support a Bolshevik revolution than was Stanley Baldwin; but the press had persuaded people that this was a Russian-inspired government of Bolsheviks and that MacDonald was planning to betray Britain to the interests of a Bolshevik revolution.

Fear of a revolution

In the twentieth century there were three periods during which it was possible to imagine that a workers' revolution was being planned. Between 1910 and 1914 the larger, militant unions organised a series of nation-wide strikes to force employers to concede better wages and working conditions. The sight of 100,000 men marching to Tower Hill to listen to Ben Tillett in 1912 was calculated to rouse the fears of the respectable middle class. In this period the government, acting on the advice of the Home Secretary, Winston Churchill, called in the Army and Navy to break the strikes. One reaction to this show of force was for the workers to form their own stronger units and the Miners' Union, Transport Workers' Union and Railway Workers' Union formed the Triple Alliance in 1913–14. This loose Alliance was to be called into play whenever one of the unions involved was in conflict with the employers. Each union promised to consult the others and promised that if necessary the three would take combined action to force the employers to concede to the union's demands. So a railway company's refusal to concede a pay increase could lead to a strike by coal miners and transport workers, not for any gain for themselves, but in support of the railwaymen. This meant that

39 The great transport strike, 28 May, 1912. The picture shows meat vans under police escort passing through the East End of London on their way to Smithfield Market. This transport strike was the first national strike ever organised by a union and was the forerunner of the post-1914 development of huge strikes by militant and growing unions. The 'respectable' classes were frightened at this development which they feared might turn into revolution

workers no longer thought of fighting their own employers but now began to think of fighting the employing class as a whole.

This Alliance came about because of the influence of the syndicalists whose belief was that the workers in each industry should take over that industry and run it for themselves, without any 'boss' class and without any profit motive being called into play.

After the war the country suffered from the anti-Bolshevik fever we have already seen in Chapter 6. Lloyd George in particular felt that the Bolshevik Revolution of 1917, which had taken Russia out of the war against Germany, was a betrayal and a menace. He called on the electorate to vote for the Party which would ensure that such a menace never threatened this country.

Meanwhile the workers had resurrected the Triple Alliance. The government had taken control of the nation's coal mines during the war to ensure the safe and continued delivery of this vital product to the armaments factories. This, the miners believed, was a step towards the permanent nationalisation of the coal industry, something which they had advocated for many years and which *Labour and the New Social Order* had proclaimed as a major part of Labour's policies. However, when the coal industry, along with most other industries, began to suffer from a slump in 1921, the government found itself having to face the possibility of paying out a subsidy to maintain the miners' wage rates. Lloyd George was unwilling to do this and promptly handed the mines back to their owners. Faced with the problem of falling sales and lower profits they announced drastic wage cuts. On 31 March 1921 the miners called on their colleagues in the Triple Alliance while starting their own strike on 1 April, 1921. However, the miners' leaders were divided; some of them indicated that they might be prepared to call off their strike if the mineowners asked for smaller wage cuts; this was the excuse for which Thomas of the railway workers had been waiting. He announced that the miners were prepared to settle, that there was no need for the Triple Alliance to come into play, and called off the threatened strike. The miners, who stayed out on strike until 1 July, felt that they had been betrayed on 'Black

40 Miners' Union leaders in 1926. Herbert Smith (left), the Union President, with General Secretary, A. J. Cook (centre), and Richardson (right), arriving at Downing Street for discussions with the Prime Minister, Stanley Baldwin. Cook was the author of the miners' slogan, 'Not a minute on the day, not a penny off the pay'

Friday'. It was, however, less a betrayal than the result of the failure of union leaders—including the miners'—to work out the full implication of their Alliance. Did they mean to call a General Strike? If so, who would call it? Who was to decide whether the striking workers' claims had been met by an employer's offer? The unions never set up any joint machinery to help run their Alliance, which remained a very loose and uncertain affair, dependent on the attitudes of individual union leaders.

Events leading to the General Strike

The failure of the MacDonald government and the continuation of a high level of unemployment created a situation in which, once again, the wilder extremists could talk about a workers' revolution. Since there was no justice to be got from the politicians, the workers would have to take matters into their own hands, use their industrial power to force employers and, if need be, the government to listen to their demands for work, higher wages and social improvements. These were the themes of speeches being made by A. J. Cook, the miners' leader, and other extremists, in 1925 and 1926.

The coal industry was particularly hard hit during the depression of the 1920s (and 1930s). Increasing foreign competition from more efficient, mechanised mines in Poland, Germany, France and the USA, meant that less British coal would have been sold anyhow. On top of this, however, there were a number of technological developments which meant that the post-war world required less coal than it had done in 1913. Oil-fired shipping, the spread of the use of electricity in the home and the factory, the development of more efficient domestic grates were only three of these developments.

The mineowners believed that the solution to the problem was simple. British coal was not being bought because it was dearer than foreign coal; therefore British coal would have to become cheaper; this could be done very simply, by lowering the miners' wages yet again. On 30 June, 1925 the owners announced their proposed cuts. The miners once again appealed to their colleagues in the Triple Alliance who in turn asked the TUC to support the miners' refusal to accept the cuts. On 31 July, 1925 the government climbed down, announced the setting up of a Royal Commission to examine the state of the industry and promised that until the Commission had reported, the government would pay the owners a subsidy to ensure that wage rates could be maintained.

The extremist union leaders were delighted with this Red Friday of 1925 which had shown, they thought, that the government could be beaten. A. J. Cook told a meeting: 'I don't care a hang for any government or Army or Navy; we have already beaten not only the employers but the strongest government of modern times'. When the Royal Commission, under Herbert Samuel, reported in March 1926 that wages would have to be cut and the miners forced to work a longer day,

Cook refused to accept these findings: 'Not a penny off the pay, not a minute on the day' was the slogan he announced.

On 30 April, 1926 the owners locked their mines in the face of the miners' refusal to accept the wage cuts. On 1 May the TUC told the government that it had taken charge of the negotiations; the struggle now was not between owners and miners but between workers and the government. However, what was never cleared up was just what the miners had handed over to the TUC. Had they handed over the control of the threatened General Strike or had they handed over the right to negotiate wage rates?

The call for a General Strike to begin on 3 May was sent out; meanwhile the TUC continued to negotiate with the government:

It was now Monday, 3 May. We were approaching the most fateful decision of the whole dispute. We knew that any attempt to impose a decision on the miners would be resisted. They would say that they had been badly let down ... It would be even worse than Black Friday of 1921 ... Herbert Smith [the miners' leader] was sitting at the table, immediately opposite Pugh [the chairman of the Negotiating Committee of the TUC]. He pointed out that the miners were now actually locked out. It was impossible to contemplate a settlement in a fortnight ... There the old man sat in the centre, watchful and careful, looking over his glasses at Pugh ... While we were talking a message came to say that Baldwin wanted to see us ... Baldwin looked very troubled, and before we sat down he said that the printers had refused to print an article in one of the London papers. That was a challenge to the government and no government could go on negotiating in these circumstances ... This was a bombshell to us, as we had no knowledge whatever of the incident to which he referred ... We concluded that the incident had deliberately been used as a means of terminating the negotiations ... We made for the door somewhat perplexed, and with a feeling that we had not been treated fairly. As we were shaking hands Baldwin said, 'Goodbye Mr Pugh, you have been a brick to me, and I hope when we meet again we will meet with as friendly a spirit as we are leaving in now ...' (*From 'Men and Work' by Lord Citrine, published in 1964 by Hutchinson.*)

Strike or revolution?

To Cook and other extremists this was the beginning of the workers' revolution—although they had made no plans for the conduct of that revolution nor for what was to follow its possible successful outcome. To Thomas, Bevin and other more practical members of the TUC, the Strike was a last resort adopted by workers who saw their living standards being attacked by rising unemployment, rising prices and falling wages. They had no revolutionary ideas. They were easily frightened when they considered what they had set in motion. Was the government going to climb down in the face of the workers' threats? If so, was Britain a democracy or a state run by the workers? If the government would not climb down, indeed from a constitutional point of view could not be expected to climb down, how were the TUC to end what they had begun? As the editor of the *Daily Herald* recalled:

> The Archbishop of Canterbury's sermon on the wireless this evening was a really moving appeal. He was down on those who talked about carrying on the struggle 'to the bitter end'. He was emphatic in his declaration that there should be no thought of making workers endure worse conditions of life. For the first time in its history, I think, the Church of England has put itself on the side of the People against the Privileged Class. The old Archbishop has been splendid.
>
> Very different the pronouncement of Cardinal Bourne that 'the General Strike is a sin against Almighty God'. Five Labour MPs—John Scurr, H. Murnin, J. Tinker, M. Conolly and J. Sullivan—who are members of the Catholic Church, have sent a letter to the Cardinal saying that they are 'seriously disturbed' by this.

Politicians and the strike

While this was going on, what was the Labour Party about? Thomas and some other leaders were MPs; they and their political colleagues realised the full implications of the Strike—which happened to be taken against a Tory government, but might so easily be taken against a Labour government at some future date. Thomas and his political colleagues were constitutionalists with a respect for the slow but sure way in which the political system worked and a horror of the revolutionary and bloody way in which extreme activity worked in, for example, Russia.

The condemnation by Cardinal Bourne and the announcement by a leading Liberal lawyer that the Strike was probably treasonable, added to the confusion in the minds of many leaders of the TUC. They received no support from their parliamentary colleagues and although the Strike was well supported Lord Citrine, in *Men and Work*, recalls that on 12 May, 1926:

> Thomas and I went to Downing Street in his car. On the road we passed Wellington Barracks, and saw troops drawn up on the parade ground. Some

The end of the General Strike: **41** J. Bromley (left) and A. B. Swales (right), members of the council of the TUC, leaving Number 10 Downing Street after seeing Stanley Baldwin **42** Labour's first woman Cabinet Minister, Margaret Bondfield, leaving Downing Street **43** Ernest Bevin, the Secretary of the Transport and General Workers' Union, after the interview with Baldwin which ended the Strike. Bevin never forgot the abysmal failure of the General Strike **44** Mrs Winston Churchill, wife of the militant Chancellor of the Exchequer, congratulating the Prime Minister, who was on his way to the House of Commons to announce the end of the Strike

LEAVING THE PREMIER'S RESIDENCE AFTER THE INTERVIEW: MR. J. BROMLEY (LEFT) AND MR. A. B. SWALES, MEMBERS OF THE COUNCIL OF THE TRADES UNION CONGRESS.

A MEMBER OF THE T.U.C. COUNCIL: MARGARET BONDFIELD LEAVING NO DOWNING STREET.

were practising with machine guns; others had gas masks on, while some were in full marching kit. A number of tanks were being overhauled with their guns grinning ominously outwards on the public . . . Arrived at Downing Street, we walked along the corridor, and Pugh said to me 'I wonder how long we are going to grovel on our hands and knees to the miners'. It was evident that he was fed up . . .

We adjourned to the Cabinet room, which only a few days before we had left with all the anxieties of the Strike before us. Now we were going to declare it at an end. Facing us, Baldwin, rather haggard and drawn . . . welcomed us with obvious anxiety. He said, 'Mr Pugh, would you be good enough to make any statement you desire?' Then Pugh announced the calling-off of the Strike, and said it had been dictated by considerations not of weakness, but of a genuine desire for peace and to allow negotiations to proceed. He was followed by Thomas, who made an eloquent appeal for better feelings. Baldwin replied, 'I thank God for your decision', and the relief that went through him and the others was very noticeable.

Unions and the future

Bevin and other, younger leaders of the trade union movement learned their lesson from the failure of the Strike to achieve anything. In future, they determined, unions would concentrate on dealing with the employers in single industries or groups of industries, negotiating on behalf of their own members and not try to challenge governments.

Reluctantly, Bevin and his colleagues, eleven of whom were trusted politicians, came to see that if workers' conditions were to be improved it would be done either by union bargains with employers or by legislation passed by governments favourable to the workers. This caused them once again to turn to political activity and in 1929 the Labour Party won 287 seats, becoming, for the first time, the largest party in the Commons, although still not having an overall majority as the Tories had 260 seats, while the Liberals had 59. Once again, MacDonald and his colleagues were asked to form a government without having any real power.

8   The Crisis of 1931

The government and unemployment

Margaret Bondfield, the first woman to be a Cabinet Minister, had declared that a Labour government would 'cure unemployment in three weeks'. One of MacDonald's first steps was to appoint J. H. Thomas as Lord Privy Seal with special responsibility for seeking a remedy to the problem of unemployment. One of the Junior Ministers who helped him was Oswald Mosley.

But far from curing unemployment the government found that the number of unemployed continued to grow from just over one million in 1929 to over 3 million in the summer of 1931. Mosley, acting on his own, produced a series of documents outlining policies which, he claimed, would create work and help at least to stem the rise in the level of unemployment. His ideas were similar to those being put forward by J. M. Keynes, the economist.

Similar ideas had been adopted by Roosevelt in the USA and by Hitler in Germany, and helped to bring down the levels of unemployment in both these countries. But the Labour Chancellor, Philip Snowden, was a traditionalist who believed that the Budget should be balanced each year, whereas Mosley's policies depended on a government being prepared to spend more than it collected in taxation, making up the difference by borrowing (as it has to do in wartime). Snowden would not accept this and his influence in the Cabinet was sufficient to ensure that Mosley's policies were rejected. Mosley resigned and took his case to the Annual Party Conference. Here the leaders of the Party argued against him but in a vote of just over two million Mosley was defeated by only 205,000 votes. If some, at least, of the Party's leaders had stood out against Snowden it is possible that Mosley and his policies might have won. As it was, Mosley left the Labour Party and went on to form his own political party which ultimately became the British Fascist Party.

The Gold Standard

The Bank of England, then a private institution with private shareholders, eager to make a profit, held the country's gold deposits which grew as foreign countries paid for British exports and which were depleted as British importers brought in foreign goods which had to be paid for in gold. Another way in which the level of gold deposits could be increased was by the Bank of England borrowing from foreign banks; in turn, it could make a profit by lending its gold to other foreign banks.

45 A Liberal Party poster for the 1929 election showing Lloyd George's determination to attack poverty; few people believed him any more. Those who wanted reform preferred to trust the Labour Party, to which Lloyd George's Liberals offered their support after the election was over

ATTACK POVERTY

THE
LIBERAL POLICY

In the 1920s the Bank of England had found it very profitable to lend gold to German and Austrian banks. These took British gold, promising to repay it in, say, 10 years or so (a long-term loan) and paid 8 per cent interest each year. The Bank of England, meanwhile, borrowed money from the French and American banks for only 2 per cent interest—but promising to repay them whenever they wanted the money back (a short-term loan). This was very profitable for the shareholders of the Bank, who were getting the benefit of the difference between an 8 per cent and a 2 per cent rate of interest. It was, however, very dangerous since the Bank would run into difficulties if the French and American banks came and asked for their money back; the Bank of England could not, in turn, ask the Germans and Austrians for a return of the money which it had given them on long-term loans.

The economic crisis

In February 1931 Snowden appointed a Committee under Sir George May to examine the possibility of the government making economies which would make it easier for Snowden to balance his Budget—that is, to spend only as much as he collected in tax each year. Parliament adjourned on 30 July, 1931 and on 1 August the May Committee announced its findings. It calculated that there would be a Budget deficit of £170 million—that is, the government was going to

The National government

Why did MacDonald decide to accept the King's invitation to remain as Prime Minister leading a Coalition government? In the mythology of the Labour Party this has always been portrayed as the great betrayal of the Party by its leaders. Today, as a result of the research of Mr Reginald Bassett we know that this was no betrayal but an attempt by MacDonald to preserve the reputation and standing of the Party.

What could he have done? He might have resigned—and the Labour Party would have been accused of running away from a major economic problem. If he had done so the electorate would, rightly, have decided that the Party could never provide men strong enough and willing enough to deal with difficult situations.

MacDonald was determined to force the Party to accept its part in working out a solution for the country's problems. He realised that this would not be popular with everyone in the Party—and he went out of his way to warn younger Ministers, such as Shinwell and Morrison, to resign, not to accept office in the National government, so that they at least would be acceptable to the Party's workers in the country.

48 Herbert Morrison at the official opening of Waterloo Bridge. The 1931 election had seen the Labour Party routed by the National government. Morrison, a Cabinet Minister 1929–31, organised the London Labour Party which, under his direction, won the London County Council elections. This gave Labour a renewed confidence and also provided many future Labour MPs with their first experience of public administration

Why did he remain as Prime Minister? In his *Autobiography*, Morrison gives the clue when he talks about the King's invitation to MacDonald:

On MacDonald's sudden and—to his colleagues—unannounced decision to desert the Labour Party I thought, and still think, that King George V was mistaken in taking the course he did by inviting—or did he urge?—MacDonald to become Prime Minister in a Coalition. The natural constitutional course for him to have taken was to ask Baldwin as leader of the Conservative Party to form a government with Liberal support, which would almost certainly have been forthcoming. As it was, the action of the King was conducive to a split in the Labour Party even though the numbers which went with MacDonald were very few ... It has been urged on the other side that he had been advised to take this course by Baldwin and Sir Herbert Samuel (and presumably MacDonald) and that he was thus taking the advice of distinguished privy councillors. I have no doubt that the King was perfectly aware of his direct responsibility and felt that the Throne should at a time of such crisis play a more direct role than was normal in easier times.

49 The National government, 1931, in the gardens of 10 Downing Street, *Standing:* (left to right) Sir Philip Cunliffe, J. H. Thomas, Lord Reading, Neville Chamberlain, Sir Samuel Hoare; *Sitting:* (left to right) Philip Snowden, Stanley Baldwin, Ramsay MacDonald, Sir Herbert Samuel, Lord Sankey

One alternative would have been for the King to ask Baldwin to become Prime Minister—but it is unlikely that the Liberals would have agreed to serve under him. Another alternative was to ask Lloyd George to form a government—but it is almost certain that the Tories would have refused to serve under him.

Coalition and the Gold Standard

MacDonald was expelled from the Labour Party on 31 August, 1931 and Henderson became leader of the parliamentary Labour Party. Meanwhile, the National government tried to put into practice the cuts recommended by the May Committee. Public servants (such as teachers) had their salaries cut by 10 per cent; unemployment benefit was cut by 10 per cent. On 15 September the sailors at Invergordon, angered at their cut in pay, refused to put to sea. This further disturbed foreign confidence in Britain and banks continued to withdraw their gold from the Bank of England. On 21 September the government announced that Britain was leaving the Gold Standard, the system by which each country settled its international trading debts by making payments in gold, the only form of international currency. This system had been suspended between 1914 and 1925, when Britain went back on to the Gold Standard and announced that in future the pound sterling would be worth $4.80, compared with the $4.02 which it had proved to be worth while the Gold Standard was suspended. The following example shows the effect of this revaluation of the pound. Assume that the price of a British car was £200 in 1925.

When the exchange rate was $4.02 to £, price in USA = $804

After revaluation, the rate was $4.80 to £, price in USA = $960

One effect of this revaluation was to increase the price of British exports so that exporters (of coal, steel, machinery etc) found it increasingly difficult to sell British goods abroad and British workers found it increasingly hard to find jobs. After September 1931 the value of the pound fell, export prices fell and British trade had a chance to recover.

When Beatrice Webb heard that Britain was leaving the Gold Standard she exclaimed: 'No one told us that this could be done'. Indeed, the crisis of 1931 had been due to the widely-held belief that gold was a sacred cow which could not be meddled with. People had prophesied all sorts of terrible calamities if Britain should leave the Gold Standard. That is what the May Committee, the Cabinet's split and the government's resignation had been all about. And yet on 21 September, all this was shown to have been pointless.

The October election 1931

It is easy to justify MacDonald's decision to form and lead a Coalition government. It is less easy to justify his decision to call for a general election in October 1931—when, incidentally, the Coalition had failed to do what it had been set up to do—namely, to preserve the pound and the Gold Standard. This was a bitterly

From the painting by Harold Speed.

NO MORE SOCIALIST PROMISES FOR ME, I'M VOTING FOR THE CONSERVATIVE NATIONAL GOVERNMENT

50 A poster issued by the National government for the 1931 election

51 Emanuel Shinwell had been a friend and colleague of Ramsay MacDonald's. In the 1935 general election Shinwell opposed MacDonald in the Seaham constituency. The picture shows Shinwell (with hat raised) being chaired by his supporters after the result had been declared on 16 November; in a sensational victory he had defeated the Prime Minister by over 20,000 votes. Labour was on the march again

fought election, with accusations of betrayal coming from one side, with Snowden leading the attack on the Labour Party:

> I hope you have read the election programme of the Labour Party. It is the most fantastic and impracticable programme ever put before the electors. All the derelict industries are to be taken over by the State, and the taxpayer is to shoulder the losses. The banks and financial houses are to be placed under national ownership and control, which means, I suppose, that they are to be run by a joint committee of the Labour Party and the Trade Union Council. Your investments are to be ordered by some board, and your foreign investments are to be mobilised to finance this madcap policy. This is not socialism. It is Bolshevism run mad.

The National government won a massive majority with 553 seats (472 Conservatives, 68 Liberals and 13 Labour followers of MacDonald). Labour had only 52 seats and Lansbury was the only ex-Minister to win a seat.

In 1935 Lansbury was forced to resign over the issue of German rearmament and Clement Attlee was chosen to lead the still small Party into the election of 1935.

The Road to Power, 1935–1951

Attlee as Party Leader

Attlee, a middle-class lawyer educated at a public school, became leader of a party which represented the trade union movement and the depressed working classes of Britain. A Tory member of the Commons recalled:

When Attlee was elected Leader of the Labour Party in 1935 . . . Hugh Dalton wrote in his diary, 'A little mouse shall lead them' . . . It is fashionable nowadays to decry the malaise and impotence of the thirties as due to the ineffectual leadership of Baldwin, MacDonald and Chamberlain . . . But Attlee had his responsibility too. After he became leader he consistently led the Labour Opposition into voting against the defence programme and Service estimates. While voicing demands for tough action against Mussolini over Abyssinia, against France during the Spanish Civil War, and against Hitler's Third Reich, at the same time he attacked our defence plans and did his utmost to frustrate rearmament, as I can testify from first-hand experience as Air Minister. Attlee's theme song was collective security . . . and he excused his votes against the Service and defence plans on the grounds that he could not accept them because he could not trust the government's foreign policy.

These facts must be stated in order to get the events of the thirties into per-

52 Dick Crossman (leaning on the gate) canvassing in the Oxford by-election in 1938—the first held after the Munich agreement between Chamberlain and Hitler. Crossman was one of the many middle-class intellectuals who joined the Labour Party in the 1930s in the hope that it would help create a better world

53 Winston Churchill (seated fifth from left) invited Bevin (far left, seated) Attlee (fourth from left, seated), Anthony Greenwood (second from right, seated), Herbert Morrison (behind Churchill) and other Labour MPs to join with him in a Coalition government

spective. Attlee represented the mood of the Labour Party at the time just as much as Baldwin and Chamberlain personified the mood of public opinion . . . Even so it was to Attlee's credit that he moved the Labour Party from its traditional pacifist posture to a greater recognition of the challenge of the age, and this made it easier for him to lead Labour into the Coalition under Churchill. (*From 'Sixty Years of Power' by the Earl of Swinton and James Margach, published in 1966 by Hutchinson.*)

Wartime government

In 1939 Britain declared war on Hitler and by May 1940 the Chamberlain government had shown itself incapable of waging war effectively. Chamberlain invited Attlee to join a Coalition government but when Attlee refused, Chamberlain resigned to make way for Winston Churchill who invited Attlee and Greenwood to enter his small War Cabinet of five; Morrison became Home Secretary, Dalton, Alexander and Jowitt became Ministers and Ernest Bevin, not then an MP, was invited to become Minister of Labour. As his biographer, Alan Bullock recalls:

On the day Bevin's appointment as Minister of Labour was announced, the *Daily Express* described him as a 'bad mixer, a good hater, respected by all' . . . No trade union leader can expect to be popular, and the press delighted to draw an unflattering picture of the trade union boss dictating to the public as well as to members of his own union. His rise in the trade union movement . . . had left him with plenty of enemies . . . In politics, the episode most commonly recalled and always held against him was the attack he had made on Lansbury at the 1935 Conference, in which the standard adjective applied to Bevin's behaviour was 'brutal' . . . Bevin did nothing to placate his critics. Where he felt strongly about an issue he expressed himself forcefully . . . When he fought he fought hard and to win. You only had to look at Ernie Bevin to see all this expressed in his physical appearance; the heavy build, big head, broad face, the obvious strength of his hands and shoulders, combined with a harsh, powerful voice and a rolling walk reminiscent of a battleship in heavy seas. 'He would square up to anyone', Attlee wrote, 'physically or morally, with relish!' 'Like Churchill,' *The Times* said, in a leading article at the time of his death, 'he seemed a visitor from the eighteenth century'. (*From the 'Life and Times of Ernest Bevin, Vol. I', published by Heinemann.*)

Labour and the war

As in the First World War (Chapter 5) thousands of trade union officials played an active part in councils and committees set up to help run the war machine. After 1940 there was no unemployment and families which had had no wage-earner in the 1930s now found themselves with, perhaps, two or three wage-earners. Though there was little on which they could spend this money in wartime, they did understand that employment was better than being workless, that money could be earned, and, in peacetime, could be spent. Their expectations were heightened; their 'poverty of desire' was chipped away and they looked forward to the peacetime in which full employment might be maintained.

The Coalition government did much to increase the workers' expectations. As Pauline Gregg reports:

The Coalition government in which the Conservatives held the majority . . . contrived to tend the flame of social reform and had produced a social programme of which any peacetime Ministry might by proud . . . It had set on foot the Beveridge Committee, a Committee on the coal industry, and a Population Commission . . . It had established the Ministry of National Insurance, whose name alone sounded a new note, and had passed two further Acts of major importance—an Education Act and the Family Allowance Act. It had, moreover, devised a scheme of demobilisation which was already beginning to operate.

54 A mock election result—one of the many such mock elections held in service camps all over the world while the war was on. This one (from Egypt) shows that many members of the forces had already made up their minds to vote Labour as soon as they had a chance

It had also produced a series of White Papers, outlining the policies which post-war governments might be expected to follow on full employment, housing, New Towns, and so on. Above all it had established the Beveridge Committee whose Report had become a best-seller and whose recommendations were so warmly welcomed. Beveridge named the Five Giant Evils which affected working-class life—Poverty, Squalor, Idleness, Illness and Ignorance—and in each case outlined policies by which each of these Evils could be attacked so that the mass of the people could lead decent lives in decent conditions.

The government had established the Army Bureau for Current Affairs which sent out young officers to lead discussion groups and debating societies, to produce pamphlets and newspapers for the members of the forces. In these papers, discussions and societies, men learned to understand Beveridge and to realise that the depressed 1930s need not be the normal pattern of life in an industrialised society.

At home, children and their parents were evacuated and middle-class people in small suburban towns took in the children from the inner city slums. For the first time these middle-class voters were brought face to face with the results of the low standard of living suffered by the poor. Many of them were converted to the idea that State action should be taken to ensure that these conditions were changed.

Election 1945

The war with Germany ended in May 1945. Churchill wanted to retain his Coalition government at least until Japan had been defeated but the Labour Party Conference, meeting at Brighton in June 1945, advised its leaders that they should resign from the Coalition and prepare to fight a post-war election against the Tories.

On 15 June Parliament was dissolved; polling day was fixed for 5 July but the declaration of the poll was fixed for 26 July, to allow the votes of the forces scattered throughout the world to be counted.

Few people believed that the Labour Party could win. Herbert Morrison was one who did. Later, he wrote:

Political myopia is the only diagnosis that can be given to the Tories' utter

55 The Labour government, 1945, with Attlee (seated, centre) flanked by Bevin (on his right) and Morrison (on his left) the architects of a social revolution

ignorance of the new outlook of the people. Counting on winning solely through the nation's admiration for its war leader, the Tories offered nothing but idol-worship and a programme of negation, plus some absurd scares.

One of the most important features of the 1945 election was the proxy vote . . . The *Daily Mirror* published a letter (from a woman reader) which said 'I shall vote for him' referring to the hopes of her soldier-husband for a better Britain, and so began a campaign built round the slogan 'Vote for Him'. It . . . undoubtedly influenced large numbers of women, who had hitherto imagined that politics were of no importance to them, to think about them and to discuss the subject in their letter to their husbands. (*From 'An Autobiography' by Herbert Morrison, published by Odhams Books.*)

Sir William Beveridge recalled:

1945 reproduced the coupon conditions of 1918, with the election at the earliest possible moment, featuring Churchill as the war winner who should be allowed to finish the job, making election day as far as possible another VE day. Why had the 1918 coupon succeeded but the 1945 coupon crashed completely? At the end of the First War we thought of going back to the good old times. During the Second War we realised that we must go forward and not back, because the times between the wars were not good.

The view of Conservative organisers is that it is easier for voters to be persuaded to vote against something than to be persuaded to vote for anything. Clearly, the people of the country were determined to vote against the Conservatives on this occasion.

In the event, the election of 1945 is one of the most remarkable in history.

They have acted on the advice which I gave in the first of my campaign speeches at Manchester, that a vote of a general election was not a vote of thanks to anyone for having led us to victory. They have shown that they wanted Churchill for war, but most emphatically did not want him, or any of his friends, for peace. (*From 'Power and Influence' by William Beveridge, published by Hodder and Stoughton.*)

When the votes were counted the Labour Party had won a record number of seats—more even than the Liberals had won in their 1906 triumph. Attlee went to Buckingham Palace to accept the King's invitation to become Prime Minister.

Labour's social revolution

Between 1945 and 1950 the Labour government carried out most of the detailed programme of reforms which it had presented to the electorate in 1945. Its most popular measures concerned the social services. Beveridge's schemes for social insurance were implemented by a string of legislation in the years 1945–48 and Nye Bevan introduced the National Health Service, perhaps the most important of all Labour's reforms. The school-leaving age was raised to fifteen, fees were abolished in local authority schools and scholarships to universities were expanded. By its legislation for town and country planning, for New Towns and for National Parks the government showed a concern for the environment.

Much of Labour's nationalisation plan was carried out. Coal and the railways, electricity and gas, road haulage and iron and steel, the Bank of England and the civil airways organisations were among those which were taken from private enterprise and entrusted to public ownership.

In spite of the problems created by the war, and its destructive effects, the government was determined to carry out its programme, basic to which was the

56 Aneurin Bevan had been a radical critic of the pre-war and wartime governments. Attlee gave him the post of Minister of Health in his government. He was the creator of the National Health Service as well as being Minister in charge of housing. He hoped to be the creator of a new society typified by the model of the new residential area which he is examining

maintenance of full employment and the raising of people's living standards. Government money was poured into the building of New Towns and housing, private enterprise was encouraged to spend money on building up the old and developing new industries, where possible, in areas which had once been depressed. Oil refineries, chemical plants, synthetic fibre producing factories were among those which were developed at this time and provided work for hundreds of thousands of people.

Taxation

However, all this cost money and the levels of direct and indirect taxation remained very high. At the same time the government maintained the wartime system of controls, licences and rationing to ensure that the most urgent things were done, that imports (even of food) were held down so that more important things (such as raw materials and machinery) could be brought in. This affected the middle class more than the workers. Press campaigns, particularly that organised by the *Daily Express* and its Housewives' League, were mounted to draw attention to shortages and rising prices, austerity and high taxation.

Election, 1950

In February 1950 Attlee called a general election. A Tory could claim, as Robert Boothby admitted, 'that the country had gone through the greatest social revolution in its history'. The economy was restored, unemployment had been abolished, the Welfare State had been created and a fairer society had been established.

The Labour government had not lost a single by-election in the five years since 1945 and at the election raised thirteen and a quarter million votes—the highest number ever recorded by a party in peacetime. This was nearly one million more votes than were cast for the Tories, but the Labour Party still lost a number of seats. With 315 seats it had an overall majority of only six.

The second Attlee government

The government which had been elected in 1945 had carried out most of its programme by 1949. Elected again in 1950 there seemed little for it left to do; it had run out of steam and had nothing further to offer. The middle class who had voted Labour in 1945 in the hope that social reform would follow, now wanted a government which would end austerity, lower taxation and allow the people freedom to enjoy their own lives.

The 1950 government was made up of the same men as had governed from 1945. They were not only older men than they had been but many of them were also sick men: Cripps had been worn out by the problem of righting the economy of the country; Bevin had spent himself in opposing Russian policies in Europe and at the UNO. When Cripps resigned in October 1950, Attlee appointed a young Minister—Hugh Gaitskell—to take his place. Gaitskell accepted Attlee's policy for rearmament at the cost of £1,500,000,000 a year. To get this money for defence Gaitskell had to cut down the money spent on welfare. One of his policies was to impose charges for dental treatment and for prescriptions. Nye Bevan, annoyed by the promotion of the young Gaitskell, resigned from the Cabinet, taking with him a young Minister, Harold Wilson who, along with John Freeman, resigned in protest against the betrayal of socialism as they understood it.

A divided party can never hope to do as well as a united party; a party which has not much idea of what its future policies should be has not as much chance as one which is eagerly getting on with implementing well thought-out and needed reforms. On top of this the Labour government found itself humiliated abroad when the Persian government nationalised the British oilfields in Persia. The patriotic press made much of this sign of Labour's weakness.

Election, 1951

In October 1951 Attlee decided to call a general election. Once again the Labour Party increased its total poll; so, too, did the Tories, and the Labour government was overthrown, the Tories having an overall majority of seventeen seats. After six years of power and after carrying through a massive series of social reforms Attlee and his colleagues had to take their place on the Opposition benches, as Churchill and the Tories entered upon the task of governing a modern, booming, prosperous Britain.

57 From left to right are Harold Wilson, Aneurin Bevan, Tom Driberg, Ian Mikardo and Barbara Castle, pictured on the eve of the 1951 Labour Party Conference at which they were going to oppose Hugh Gaitskell's policies on taxation and the financing of the Health Service

10 Tory Socialism and a New-look Labour Party, 1951-1970

Tory socialism

In 1955 Sir Winston Churchill resigned to make way for Sir Anthony Eden (later Lord Avon), whose Suez adventure in 1956 led to his resignation and after which Harold Macmillan became Prime Minister. Under Churchill and Eden, R. A. Butler had been Chancellor and his policies had been so similar to those followed by his Labour predecessor, Hugh Gaitskell, that journalists coined the word 'Butskellism' to describe the Tory Party's policies. As Harold Macmillan wrote in his memoirs:

> It is very difficult for those whose memories do not go back to the twenties and thirties to have any conception of the virulence with which the role of the State in a modern economy was contested . . . Any form of State intervention was believed to be necessarily incompetent, and the prelude to some form of dictatorship. Some of the most intelligent and responsible leaders in many fields of national life had supported *laissez-faire* on these grounds . . .

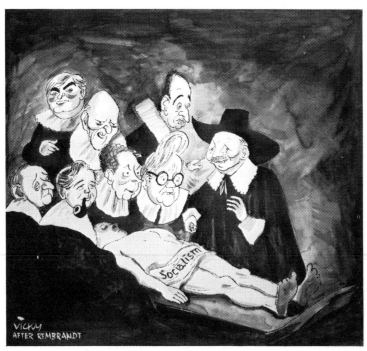

58 Attlee (far right, in hat), Morrison (with glasses) and Gaitskell (on Morrison's right) were, according to the cartoonist Vicky, responsible for the death of socialism. Harold Wilson (with pipe), Shinwell (on his left) and Bevan (far left), do not seem unduly worried at this development in the Labour Party's fortunes

Nevertheless, much of what I was advocating in those years has come about; a National Economic Development Council; a government which controls the Central Bank, and assumes responsibility for the general level of economic activity through the Bank rate and the Budget; extensions of the public utility principle in transport and fuel; even some welfare distribution of essential foods, such as the expanded schools meals service and the orange juice and cod-liver oil and milk for mothers and babies. The era of strict *laissez-faire* has passed into history, together with the derelict towns, the boarded-up shops, and the barefooted children and—above all—the long rows of men and women outside the Labour Exchanges. (*From 'Winds of Change', 1966 published by Macmillan.*)

The Tories governed a Britain that was booming as it had never done before. As Macmillan said in July 1957:

When I first stood for the House of Commons in 1923, and for the next fifteen years, one problem only held the political field. The problem of rapidly falling prices and massive unemployment. We debated it week by week. We put forward all kinds of rival views as to how it should be solved. Today, it has solved itself. Every Hon Member knows that for the mass of the people there has never been such a good time or such a high standard of living. I repeat what I said at Bedford, they have 'never had it so good'.

The electorate in the booming, affluent Britain was satisfied. David Butler reported in 1960:

High incomes have enabled most of the British people to enjoy a way of life that was inconceivable in the 1930s and unobtainable in the 1940s. Increasingly, the largest firms were mass-producing goods appealing to working-class as well as to the middle-class people. The mass consumption of goods has helped to lessen old class distinction based on housing, dress and means of travel. Less than a decade previously, cars, holidays abroad and television were considered the perquisites of a minority of the middle class. Before the war in many working-class areas, the home had few amenities. An individual's life often centred around communal meeting–places—the street, the pub, the fish and chip shop, the cinema, the union, the chapel or perhaps the Co-op hall. But now, in new homes, the living-room has become more attractive than the pub, and everywhere television provides more entertainment than the cinema. A car or a motor-cycle and sidecar is a focus of family life as well as a symbol of prosperity; it is not necessary to wait for a work's charabanc trip to go to the seaside.
    A significant number of skilled workers may be called class hybrids—working class in terms of occupation, education, speech and cultural norms, while becoming middle class in terms of income and material comforts. With the disappearance of many of the most overt distinctions between middle and working class, the sense of class conflict has been reduced. (*From 'The British General Election of 1959' by Butler and Rose, published by Macmillan.*)

87

This affluent electorate was satisfied with the Tory government and, having elected one in 1951, did so again in 1955—this time with an increased majority—and did so yet again in 1959. This was the first time that a party had won three elections in a row, each time increasing its majority. It was also, of course, the first time that a party had *lost* three elections in a row. The Labour Party had lost seats in the elections of 1950, 1951, 1955 and 1959.

The new-look Labour Party

Hugh Gaitskell had succeeded Clement Attlee as Party leader in 1955 and after the 1959 election it was Gaitskell and his friends who decided that the Party would have to change its policies and its appeals to the electorate if it were to do any better in future. This led to a period of recrimination between those who, like Gaitskell, thought that the Party should give up its socialist aims of nationalisation, and those who maintained that this would be to betray all that the Party stood for. This row was deepened by the controversy over the future of Britain's nuclear deterrent. Gaitskell, seeing himself as a future Prime Minister, was anxious to get the Party to declare that it supported Britain's retention of nuclear weapons. Others, and in particular the leaders of several large trade unions, thought that Britain ought to unilaterally renounce its nuclear weapons, as advocated by the Campaign for Nuclear Disarmament (CND). In October, 1960 the Party Conference voted in favour of a CND resolution. Gaitskell aroused great controversy by declaring that he and his friends would 'fight, fight and fight again' against this policy.

59 Hugh Gaitskell, Labour's leader after Attlee's retirement, tried to change the Party's outlook on socialism and defence. His attempts only widened splits in the party which had their origins in his taxation policies in the 1950 and 1951 Budgets

60 Harold Wilson as leader of the Labour Opposition visited America in April 1963. He called on President Kennedy (left) at the White House. Wilson hoped to persuade the British electorate that he was another Kennedy-type figure—young, successful and eager to modernise the country and its industries

Was the Party Conference to decide the policies to be followed by the parliamentary Labour Party? In the Tory and Liberal Parties this issue had been fought out in the late-nineteenth century and in each case the parliamentary leaders had persuaded their rank and file supporters to give them a free hand. In the Labour Party the issue was apparently settled in 1945, when Attlee told Harold Laski (the Party Chairman) that the parliamentary Party would not be bound by Conference decisions. In 1960 Gaitskell was merely repeating what Attlee had said. But because of the rank and file suspicion that Gaitskell was preparing to betray socialism by renouncing the 1918 constitution over nationalisation, they tried to force the Party to declare that the Conference was the decision-making body while the parliamentary Party was merely the organ for carrying out the policies determined by Conference.

Wilson and the modern party
Hugh Gaitskell died in 1963 and was succeeded by Harold Wilson. One advantage he enjoyed was that left wingers remembered his resignation from the Labour government in 1951 over the issue of rearmament and prescription charges. He stood to the left of centre in the Party's thinking while Gaitskell had inclined more to the right. Frank Cousins and other left-wing trade union leaders were more likely to support Wilson than Gaitskell.

Another advantage he enjoyed was that he refused to tackle problems head-on, as Gaitskell had done. Should the Party give up its pledges on nationalisation? Gaitskell wanted the Conference to agree to this. Wilson didn't raise the issue—he just let it die out so that there was no controversy inside the Party.

But Wilson's major advantage was that he became Party leader at the time when the Tory Party's popularity was falling. The economic boom engineered by Macmillan in 1958 and 1959 petered out into the credit squeeze organised by Selwyn Lloyd in 1961. This in turn led to unemployment and a series of by-election defeats for the Tory Party. David Butler reported:

The government's electoral battering early in 1962 gave rise to rumours that Mr Macmillan intended to reshuffle his Cabinet. On 12 July at Leicester North-West the Conservative candidate finished an ignominious third, 10 per cent behind the Liberal. The next day the Chancellor of the Exchequer was sacked, along with the Lord Chancellor and five other Cabinet Ministers. Many believed Macmillan was 'mainly acting in desperation because of the government's recent by-election defeats'.

The government was equally concerned with the problems of relations with Europe. In December 1962 Mr Macmillan discussed the faltering Common Market negotiations with President de Gaulle, who, on 14 January, 1963, indicated that his country could no longer support Britain's application for EEC membership.

Meanwhile, Britain was enduring the worst winter since 1881. The economy had been slack throughout 1962. Now bad weather led to mounting unemployment. The number of unemployed rose to 2.5 per cent of the labour force in December 1962 (compared with 1.7 per cent a year earlier); in February 1963 the total reached 3.9 per cent, the highest figure since the fuel crisis of 1947. The number who feared unemployment was even higher, 19 per cent of a Gallup Sample [opinion poll] believed that they or a member of their family would be affected. The regions farthest from London were particularly hard hit; in February, 7 per cent of the labour force were out of work in the North-East, 6 per cent in Scotland and 6 per cent in Wales. During the late winter Conservative murmurings against Mr Macmillan's leadership could be heard.

61 A face reflected in a passing bus in February 1964. Harold Macmillan walking unheeded along Whitehall where he had so recently walked as a successful Prime Minister

62 Passengers at London Bridge station arguing with an engine driver during the strike called by Southern Region train drivers in August 1969. Labour relations were no better under Labour than they had been under the previous Conservative government

(*From 'The British General Election of 1964 by Butler and King, published by Macmillan.*)

In the 1950s nothing had succeeded like success; in the early 1960s nothing failed like failure and the government's popularity continued to fall. A change of leadership when Sir Alec Douglas Home succeeded Macmillan did not seem to make much difference. Wilson and the Labour Party seemed to be destined to win the next election.

The new classes
One of Wilson's main speeches was made in October, 1963 when he appealed to the new middle class to support the Labour Party. This new class of technologists, designers, architects, salesmen and so on, were the products of Britain's new universities, colleges of technology and the industrial boom. Wilson argued that the Tory Party—led by an aristocratic product of the public schools—was less attuned to the wishes and ambitions of the new class than was the Labour Party led by a scholarship-winning university graduate. He appealed to the new class to join with the traditional working-class supporters of the Labour Party to help them create a new Britain in which there would be economic planning, an end to credit squeezes, full employment, social justice for all and in which the Labour Party could claim 'they have never had it so good'.

This was a different appeal from that outlined in the 1918 *Labour and the New Social Order*. It was different, too, to the policies outlined in 1945, 1950 and 1955. This was a series of policies which recognised that Britain in the 1960s was no longer the depressed Britain of the 1930s or the Britain of shortages and austerity of the 1940s. In the election of 1964 this pragmatic socialism was successful, the Labour Party winning 317 seats to the 304 won by the Conservatives and the 9 won by the Liberals.

63 Vicky, the cartoonist, portrayed Wilson as President Johnson's servant. The USA influenced British policy over Vietnam, nuclear power and economic development; Labour supporters, such as Vicky, resented this

Labour, the Party of government

In March 1966 Wilson called another general election and the electors returned 363 Labour MPs 253 Tories and 12 Liberals, giving Labour an overall majority of 97 and a vote of confidence in the Labour Party over the Conservatives, now led by Edward Heath.

It is too soon to try to write a critical account of recent politics which are still clouded by controversy. What can be said is that the Labour governments of 1964–70 were faced with great problems—of inflation and balance of payments in particular—and that they tried to solve these problems as their Tory predecessors had done. Economic planning was seen to be unworkable; credit squeezes were brought in by one Labour Chancellor after another; unemployment rose to new post-war record heights; housing schemes were abandoned and plans to raise the school-leaving age were dropped.

The government claimed that it was trying to right the economy, and by 1970 it had succeeded in doing so. The balance of payments position in 1970 was the healthiest it had been for half a century. But this was not what its supporters hoped from a Labour government. A Tory government might have done exactly the same, indeed, would have been forced to do almost the same in the face of events. What was different about the Wilson government? In the opinion of many of its rank and file supporters the answer was 'Nothing'. One result of this was that in 1970 many of these did not bother to vote, while many of those voting for the first time supported the Tories led by Edward Heath who became Prime Minister in 1970.

Workers' initiative

Many workers were persuaded in 1970—as they had been in 1910, 1918 and 1926—that their best plan lay in using their industrial power, since the politicians were unable or unwilling to do much to help them. When the Tory government announced that it was not going to subsidise the Upper Clyde Shipbuilders (UCS) and that the yards of this firm would have to close, it was also announcing that about 20,000 men would lose their jobs. The workers at UCS, led by their shop stewards, refused to accept this decision and, not relying on the politicians to make out a case for them, they declared that they would take over the yards for themselves. They continued to run the yards and build ships until a satisfactory agreement was reached with an American firm who took over the yard without causing many redundancies.

Elsewhere, direct action has been seen to be more effective than political negotiation. The activities of Peter Haine and the young radicals led to the cancellation of the South African Cricket Tour in 1970—and forced the South African government to change its policies towards coloured sportsmen. Direct action by a Civil Rights Association in Northern Ireland forced the government to change its policies towards Catholics there.

In one sense this is something which Labour Party supporters should welcome—the Party, after all, stands for social justice and in South Africa, Northern Ireland and on the Clyde measures leading towards this end have been achieved. However, it has been achieved without any action by the Labour Party as such. If people are persuaded that they will get more by direct action than they can get from political action then the Labour Party may get less support in the future than in the past.

This is what lies behind the current cry in the Labour Party for it to work out new policies with a deeper socialist content which it can offer to the electorate. This would be to go back on what the Party had done in 1964 and 1966, when its appeal to the electorate was that it could run a capitalist boom more efficiently than the Tories could. Now, the Party is being asked once again to set itself up as a socialist alternative to the capitalist government led by Edward Heath. The future will tell whether the Party decides to become a socialist party or to remain a moderate alternative to the Tories.

64 Clyde shipyard workers led by Jimmy Reid and other shop stewards came to London in June 1971 to try to persuade the Conservative government to keep their yards open—and so safeguard their jobs. Labour MP Anthony Wedgwood Benn (centre), led the delegation to Downing Street—a case of the Labour politicians trying to get some credit from the direct action of the men and their stewards

Further Reading

General studies of the history of political parties

THOMAS, IVOR BULMER	*The Growth of the British Party System*	Baker
MACKENZIE, R. T.	*British Political Parties*	Heinemann
JENNINGS, SIR IVOR	*Party Politics—The Growth of Parties, Vol. 2*	C.U.P.

The Labour Party

PELLING, H.	*A Short History of the Labour Party*	Macmillan
PELLING, H. (ED) (in the British Political Tradition series)	*The Challenge of Socialism*	Black
PELLING, H.	*Origins of the Labour Party, 1880–1900*	O.U.P.
COLE, G. D. H.	*Short History of the British Working Class Movement*	Allen & Unwin

Memoirs or autobiographies

MORRISON, H.	*An Autobiography*	Odhams
ATTLEE, C. R. (ED.) F. WILLIAMS	*A Prime Minister Remembers*	Heinemann
SNOWDEN, PHILIP	*Autobiography*	Ivor Nicholson and Watson
DALTON, HUGH	*Volumes of Memoirs*	Muller

Biographies

BLAXLAND	*A Life for Unity (J. H. Thomas)*	Muller
HUGHES, E.	*Keir Hardie*	Allen & Unwin
BULLOCK, A.	*Ernest Bevin*	Heinemann
FOOT, M.	*Aneurin Bevan*	MacGibbon & Kee

Topics

SKIDELSKY, R.	*Politicians and the Slump*	Penguin
COWLING, M.	*The Impact of Labour: 1920–24; the beginnings of Modern British Politics*	
LYMAN, R. W.	*The First Labour Government*	Chapman & Hall
MIDDLEMAS, R. K.	*The Clydesiders*	Hutchinson
CHESTER, L. (et al.)	*The Zinoviev Letter*	Heinemann
SYMONS, JULIAN	*The General Strike*	Cresset
PELLING, H.	*A History of British Trade Unionism*	Macmillan
MARWICK, A.	*The Deluge: British Society and the First World War*	Bodley Head

Index

Numbers in **bold type** indicate pages on which illustrations appear